About the Authors

Denise Sutherland is an Australian puzzle writer. She has studied science, music, art, and graphic design, which helps no end when it comes to writing puzzles of all kinds. She is the author of *Word Searches For Dummies,* amongst other books, and is syndicated through Auspac Media. She lives in Canberra, the Australian capital, with her husband and kids.

When not puzzling, Denise can be found knitting obsessively and reading murder mysteries.

Mark E. Koltko-Rivera, PhD, is a writer who lives with his wife Kathleen in New York City. Mark is a 32° Scottish Rite Freemason, and a Knight Templar in the York Rite of Freemasonry. He wrote *Discovering the Lost Symbol: The Mind of Dan Brown, the Truth About the Freemasons, and the Idea that We Can Become Gods,* as well as *Freemasonry: An Introduction,* and the chapter on Freemasonry in Dan Burstein's book, *Secrets of The Lost Symbol.* Mark thanks Christopher Hodapp for recommending him for this project.

Cracking Codes & Cryptograms FOR DUMMIES®

by **Denise Sutherland**
Syndicated puzzle author

by **Mark E. Koltko-Rivera, PhD**
M.∴M.∴, 32°, KT

Foreword by Chris Hodapp
Author and coauthor of
Freemasons For Dummies
The Templar Code For Dummies
Conspiracy Theories & Secret Societies For Dummies

WILEY

Wiley Publishing, Inc.

Cracking Codes & Cryptograms For Dummies®

Published by
Wiley Publishing, Inc.
111 River Street
Hoboken, NJ 07030-5774

www.wiley.com

Copyright © 2010 by Wiley Publishing, Inc., Indianapolis, Indiana

Published by Wiley Publishing, Inc., Indianapolis, Indiana

Published simultaneously in Canada

For general information on our other products and services, please contact our Customer Care Department within the U.S. at 877-762-2974, outside the U.S. at 317-572-3993, or fax 317-572-4002.

For technical support, please visit www.wiley.com/techsupport.

Wiley also publishes its books in a variety of electronic formats. Some content that appears in print may not be available in electronic books.

Library of Congress Control Number: 2009937275

ISBN: 978-0-470-59100-0

10 9 8 7 6 5 4 3

WILEY

Dedication

Denise dedicates the book to the memory of Tony Newell, 1943–2009.

Av znkx, deiirnkx, mih askx oscrib eiqon, xmpni zndsgn lrk xran zv onepmnarm. Ksgnov arkknh.

Mark dedicates the book to Brittany, who likes to figure things out.

68.40.27.55.66.37 29.91.99.68.98 68.27.46 40.27.05.34.37 3 0.68.03.99 34.91.60.37 29.03.66.55.55.68.27.98 60.37.03.98 30.40.05.41

Publisher's Acknowledgments

We're proud of this book; please send us your comments at http://dummies.custhelp.com. For other comments, please contact our Customer Care Department within the U.S. at 877-762-2974, outside the U.S. at 317-572-3993, or fax 317-572-4002.

Some of the people who helped bring this book to market include the following:

Acquisitions and Editorial

Project Editor: Sarah Faulkner

Acquisitions Editor: Tracy Boggier

Assistant Editor: Erin Calligan Mooney

Editorial Program Coordinator:
Joe Niesen

Editorial Manager: Christine Meloy Beck

Editorial Assistants: Jennette ElNaggar,
David Lutton

Cartoons: Rich Tennant
(www.the5thwave.com)

Composition Services

Project Coordinator: Kristie Rees

Layout and Graphics: Carrie A. Cesavice,
Joyce Haughey, Erin Zeltner

Proofreader: Melissa D. Buddendeck

Publishing and Editorial for Consumer Dummies

Diane Graves Steele, Vice President and Publisher, Consumer Dummies

Kristin Ferguson-Wagstaffe, Product Development Director, Consumer Dummies

Ensley Eikenburg, Associate Publisher, Travel

Kelly Regan, Editorial Director, Travel

Publishing for Technology Dummies

Andy Cummings, Vice President and Publisher, Dummies Technology/General User

Composition Services

Debbie Stailey, Director of Composition Services

Contents at a Glance

Foreword

I believe it was Sherlock Holmes who once said, "Why, look, Watson! It's a simple English schoolboy's code! Quick, get me a simple English schoolboy!" Okay, maybe he didn't actually say that.

Puzzles frustrate me. They always have. I have a tendency to stare at puzzles, cryptograms, and coded writing until beads of blood form on my forehead. I would have made a lousy Batman — I would have let the Riddler flood Gotham City or rob Fort Knox of its gold, because there was no way I was about to decipher one of his riddled clues. There I would have sat in the Bat Cave, with beads of blood forming on my cowl.

Cryptograms and secret codes have existed for centuries — there is evidence of coded writing dating back to the ancient Egyptians. Everyone, from kings and generals to criminal masterminds and 8th-grade study-hall cheaters, have sought ways to secretly communicate with each other while preventing spies, eavesdroppers, and biology teachers from discovering their plans. Wars and civilizations have turned on whether codes and ciphers were cracked or remained hidden. The outcome of World War II hinged on the ability of the British intelligence service to decipher messages sent by Nazi Germany's famed "Enigma" machine. The U.S. military used Navajo, Cherokee, Choctaw, and Comanche "code talkers" during the war to transmit coded messages that were not based on commonly known languages and were, therefore, unbreakable.

I hadn't thought much about coded writing until I became a Freemason. Because Masons are forbidden to write down their rituals, frustrated members over the last 300 years have sought ways to create study guides so they might learn the words without actually breaking the rules. Some have simply written single-letter ciphers ("AYAM?" would stand for "Are you a Mason?"). Others got more complex, using symbols and abbreviations cribbed from old-fashioned shorthand (which is its own kind of coded writing once known by the most powerful people on Earth, secretaries and stenographers, and is today mostly a lost art). Still others came up with a whole series of coded alphabets that look like an indecipherable collection of right-angle stick figures and dots, devised from what is known in code-writing world as a *Pigpen Cipher*. In fact, this type of cipher is the centerpiece of a Masonic degree ritual called the Royal Arch Degree.

This kind of thing would have remained in the realm of a small corner of the population if it hadn't been for Dan Brown and his novels. His fictional "symbologist" Robert Langdon took the subject out of the realm of tweedy MENSA meetings and made it both entertaining and exciting. From his "ambigrams" in *Angels & Demons* and the "cryptex" of *The Da Vinci Code* to the lost symbols of, well, *The Lost Symbol,* it's not often that arcane, dusty, and obscure knowledge gets to collide head-first with mind-exercising fun in one package. It's like two mutually exclusive brains shot out of opposite sides of a particle accelerator and squashed into one terrific pile of pages, if your stomach can pardon the potentially icky metaphor.

Out of two such colliding brains comes the book you now hold. My friend Mark Koltko-Rivera is well-versed in the history, philosophy, symbolism, and methods of secret (and secretive) societies. He was hot on the trail of Dan Brown's clues from *The Lost Symbol* since the day they first appeared on the Internet in the summer of 2009, and his online blog entries about them were endlessly fascinating, exploring subjects far deeper than just the surface answers to the puzzles. Mark has a PhD in psychology and has specialized over the years in "worldviews," which are ways in which people make assumptions about reality and the effects of those assumptions. That makes him uniquely qualified to look at a code or cipher and see it differently than others do.

Denise Sutherland is a puzzle designer *extraordinaire*. Her puzzles, word searches, and designs have literally appeared all over the world, and she has an endless fascination with words. She is able to think differently about the way words can be jumbled together. Of course, she lives upside down in Australia and is married to an astrophysicist, which can only help when it comes to standing complex word combinations on their heads.

The result is a book with which I think you'll spend many happy hours engaged in frustration and surprise. As for me, I have every intention of taking this one to the beach. I'll be easy to spot. I'll be the one in a Batman suit, staring into the book with beads of blood forming on my cowl.

Chris Hodapp
Indianapolis
September 2, 2009

Introduction

*Y*ou may have picked up this book for any number of reasons. Perhaps you really like trying to crack the codes in Dan Brown's novels. Maybe you liked playing with secret decoder rings pulled from boxes of cereal as a kid. Perhaps you were the kind of person who as a youngster liked to share secret, coded messages with your friends. Then again, you may be one of the many adults who likes to exercise your brain with the challenge of making and breaking encrypted messages. Or maybe you're just a professional espionage agent who's looking for tips and some recreation. (Hey, it's a tough life. Spies need fun, too.)

In *Cracking Codes & Cryptograms For Dummies* you can find fun, recreation, challenges for your brain, and information for your mind. The puzzles in this book immerse you in a world like the one in Dan Brown's *The Lost Symbol* (published by Doubleday Books), where conspirators in the United States have labored for centuries to keep some secrets hidden dark and deep. (But can anything *stay* secret . . . ?)

About This Book

Cracking Codes & Cryptograms For Dummies offers you the chance to use cryptography, cipher keys, symbols, and codes to reveal the narrative of three conspiracy stories, piece by piece and puzzle by puzzle. In this book, *you're* the symbologist; we give you everything you need to uncover the mysteries we set up in Chapter 3, and along the way we tell you about the use of codes and cryptograms in the world of secret societies.

The great thing is that you can solve the puzzles in this book in any order. Do them just for fun at your leisure. Tackle only the Easy puzzles (or only the Treacherous puzzles if you dare!). Or work well into the night to decipher all the puzzles relating to The Conspiracy of West Point (see Chapter 3 for more about this conspiracy). If you get stuck at any point, check out the hints in Chapter 14. And don't forget to check your answers against Chapter 15.

Conventions Used in This Book

To make working through this book a little easier for you, we set some conventions early on. (We thought about *creating* a secret society and ensuring you were initiated into it before we let you in on those conventions, but then we realized that hanging you from the ceiling by your ankles as you held burning candles in each hand could get a little messy, what with the drippy wax and all. Just kidding!) Everything you need to know is right here:

- ✔ In Chapter 3, we present you with three conspiracy stories that just happen to have large chunks of text missing. At the end of each chunk of missing text, we include a puzzle number in parentheses. Find that puzzle in Part II, solve it, and write the answer into the blanks in Chapter 3.

- ✔ All puzzles in this book have a difficulty rating of Easy, Tricky, or Treacherous. Use that rating to select your preferred level of difficulty, and don't be afraid to challenge yourself from time to time!

- ✔ If you get stuck on any puzzle, regardless of difficulty level, flip to Chapter 14. There we give you a hint to help you solve each puzzle. And don't worry, the answers are in Chapter 15, so you won't accidentally see the solution when you're looking up the hint. (We would never ruin your fun like that!)

- ✔ Although some of the shorter puzzles in this book look like they're easy to solve (and some of the long puzzles look downright impossible), remember that length can be deceiving! If you don't have enough room to decipher a puzzle on any given page, we recommend using scrap paper.

What You're Not to Read

You don't have to read every single part of this book. (But if you're like us, being told by the powers-that-be that you *don't* have to read something just ensures that you'll read it.)

If you're interested only in solving some fun cryptograms, feel free to ignore the fascinating bits of secret society lore in Chapter 1. If you already know how to solve all the different puzzle varieties in this book, you can skip Chapter 2. And as with all books in the For Dummies series, this one includes gray-shaded boxes of text (called sidebars) that are filled with fun information that's ultimately inessential to understanding the topic at hand.

Foolish Assumptions

As we were writing this book, we made some assumptions about you, the reader:

- ✔ The conspiracy stories involve the fraternal group known as the Freemasons, but you don't really need to know anything about Freemasonry to enjoy the book and its puzzles. If you're curious about Freemasonry, you may want to read some of the books we suggest at the end of Chapter 1. While you're at it, check out *Conspiracy Theories & Secret Societies For Dummies* by Christopher Hodapp and Alice Von Kannon (Wiley).

- ✔ We assume you know the most basic concepts involving the American Revolutionary War and the American War between the States (the Civil War). However, if you want to discover more about these subjects — well, big surprise, we have For Dummies books for that! Consider reading *U.S. History For Dummies*, 2nd Edition, by Steve Wiegand, *U. S. Military History For Dummies* by John C. McManus, and *The Civil War For Dummies* by Keith D. Dickson (all published by Wiley).

- ✔ On the puzzle-solving front, we assume only that you're prepared to persevere with these ciphers. Many of them are easy to solve, but you may need a few tries to get some of them right.

> ✔ If you want to discover more about letter frequency
> analysis — a basic skill for solving cryptograms — you
> can delve into coauthor Denise's book *Word Searches*
> *For Dummies* (Wiley). For an academic treatise, try
> *Cryptanalysis: A Study of Ciphers and Their Solution* by
> Helen Fouché Gaines (Dover).

How This Book Is Organized

This book is divided into three parts. Read on for more
information about each.

Part I: Code and Cryptogram Strategies

We start off by giving you some background information on
codes and cryptograms, both from an historical perspective
and from a practical perspective. If you want to know what
sorts of secret codes were used during World War II, or if
you want to know how to solve a Caesar Box Cipher, head to
this part.

Part II: Secret Stories, Codes, and Cryptogram Puzzles

This part makes up the majority of the book and includes the
super-secret conspiracy stories as well as all the puzzles you
need to solve the stories! Decipher some of the additional
puzzles to discover some entertaining quotations.

Part III: Hints and Answers to the Cryptos and Codes

This part is exactly what it sounds like. Here we give you hints
and answers for all the puzzles in the book.

Icons Used in This Book

We included little pictures in the margins of this book. They aren't a secret code but a way of highlighting certain information.

The Tip icon clues you in on how to solve a puzzle or otherwise work more efficiently.

The Remember icon highlights the text you may want to refer to again and again.

The Warning icon shows you potential pitfalls to stay away from as you work through the puzzles in this book.

Where to Go from Here

You're free to read this book in any order — flip at random and see what sort of fun puzzle you land on first! You can always work backward or forward from there or continue to jump around.

If you're the logical sort who simply must start at the beginning, turn the page and discover the world of codes and cryptograms. If you want to know how to solve the specific puzzle types in this book, start with Chapter 2. And if you're looking for fun and easy letter-substitution cryptograms, go to Chapter 4 first. Finally, if conspiracy stories draw you in every time, we suggest you head immediately to Chapter 3.

Part I

Code and Cryptogram Strategies

The 5th Wave   By Rich Tennant

"Enter here? That's what they <u>want</u> you to believe."

In this part . . .

We introduce you to the world of cryptography, telling you about its history as well as its modern uses. Chapter 1 specifically highlights Masonic codes and ciphers.

In Chapter 2 we introduce you to many classic and modern types of ciphers, including some rare Masonic Ciphers that date back one or more centuries, and some new ciphers that are based on computer keyboards and cellphone keypads. Chapter 2 also contains all the instructions on how to solve the puzzles in this book.

Chapter 1

Clueing You In about Codes and Cryptograms

In This Chapter

▶ Discovering cryptography through the ages

▶ Finding out about Masonic codes and ciphers

▶ Investigating additional resources

*I*n this book, we offer you the challenge of breaking several types of real ciphers and cryptograms, all devised by noted Australian puzzlemaster Denise Sutherland (author of *Word Searches For Dummies* [Wiley]).

In this chapter, we offer a few things to orient you to the secrets of codes and cryptograms, including the world of the cryptogram, the history of ciphers and codes, and the ways in which the time-honored fraternity of the Freemasons has used codes over the centuries. We also tell you about the contemporary world of codes and follow up by giving you some suggestions for further reading.

Introducing the Cryptographic World

The word *cryptographic* comes from elements that mean "hidden" *(crypto)* and "writing" *(graph)*. The cryptographic world encompasses codes and ciphers (which we distinguish between in Chapter 2), which are used to create *cryptograms* (secret messages).

Ciphers. Codes. Cryptograms. What do you think about when you hear these words?

You may get an image of dark nights with fog-filled streets. In an attic in wartime London, a nervous man, constantly checking the door with anxious looks over his shoulder, is bent over a static-filled radio, writing down strings of numbers as they come over one particular frequency on the dial. In the street below, people in trench coats trade identical briefcases on street corners after an exchange of passwords. Such is the popular image — and, to some extent, the truth — of espionage, a world where ciphers, codes, and cryptograms are part of everyday reality.

Perhaps you prefer a more ancient or historical slant. Maybe you're thinking of Julius Caesar sending messages to his troops in the hostile wilds of Western Europe, in the years before he ruled the Roman Empire. Perhaps you wonder about the secrets encoded on parchment in the Middle Ages and during the Renaissance by people who had quite a lot to lose — like their lives: political plotters, alchemists, and even — gasp! — practitioners of magic and sorcery. And then there are the secret societies of history, some political (the Black Hand of Serbia, the Holy Vehm, the Bavarian Illuminati), some criminal (the Black Hand of Sicily, La Cosa Nostra), some religious (the Rosicrucians), some fraternal (the Freemasons and their affiliated organizations, the York and Scottish Rites).

Then again, you may prefer a more modern and military approach. Military and diplomatic ciphers can make or break a nation in wartime. Just in the relatively short period of American history, ciphers and codes have played prominent roles in the American Revolutionary War and the War Between the States, and afterward. In the world at large, codes and ciphers — which ones were broken and which ones endured — had much to do with determining the outcomes of World Wars I and II, thus affecting the lives of billions of people. Your life may have been very different if the brave geniuses of Britain's Bletchley Park group hadn't broken the German Enigma ciphers.

Of course, today cryptography has gone corporate. You probably send or receive multiple encrypted messages every business day without even knowing it, as you transfer funds from an ATM to your pocket, as you order merchandise over the Internet, even as you communicate through telephone or e-mail. Keeping these communications secure is big business — and big trouble when it fails.

Considering the History of Codes and Ciphers

The origins of codes and ciphers — like the beginnings of language and writing, and my entire Beatles LP collection — are lost in the sands of time. David Kahn, the master historian of codes and ciphers, wrote that the development of secret writing was inevitable in any literate human culture because of "the multiple human needs and desires that demand privacy among two or more people."

Then again, legends tell of another source of secret writing. In Jewish tradition, the most ancient book was written by God and delivered to Adam in the Garden of Eden by the angel Raziel (a name that means "secrets of God"). The first published edition of the *Book of Raziel the Angel* appeared in Amsterdam in 1701. One part of that book illustrates divine alphabets that could be used to encode secrets — divine or otherwise.

Parts of the Jewish Talmud (second century AD) reflect the belief that secret messages were encoded within the text of the Bible. These messages could be decoded according to specific rules, such as *gematria* (the use of the numerical equivalents of the Hebrew letters, where the first letter has the numerical value "1," and so on). The use of *gematria* and other methods to detect secret messages in the Bible appears today in the study of *Kabbalah,* one approach to Jewish mysticism. (If you're interested in discovering more about this topic, check out *Kabbalah For Dummies* by Arthur Kurzweil [Wiley].)

Whether you accept a human or a divine origin of codes and ciphers — or both! — the following sections offer you some tantalizing references to what *could* be codes and ciphers in ancient literature of a very early date.

Early ciphers

Homer's *Iliad* — thought to date between the sixth and eighth centuries BC — has exactly one reference to writing. It comes up in the story-within-a-story of Bellerophon, who was sent off by an angry monarch with folded and sealed "tablets on which he [the monarch] had traced a number of devices with a deadly meaning," tablets that Bellerophon was to give to another king, who was supposed to kill Bellerophon after reading the message. To this day, a message that instructs the recipient to kill the messenger is called a "bellerophontic" message. Is Homer's wording a fancy way to talk about normal writing — or does it indicate the use of a code or cipher? We don't know.

The earliest use of a cipher for military purposes involved the fifth century BC Spartans of Greece. They used the device called the *scytale,* a baton. A strip of paper or leather was wrapped around the baton, and the message was written straight across the different "columns" of the paper or leather. The recipient of the message would wrap the leather or paper around a baton of the same dimensions and then read the message off the material wound about the baton.

The second century BC Greek historian Polybius devised a ciphering system that has been used for centuries. Polybius put the letters of the alphabet in a 5 x 5 array like a short checkerboard. In Polybius's system, each letter is described in terms of the column and row in which it appears. Thus, "A" is ciphered as "1-1," "B" as "1-2," all the way to "Z" as "5-5." (In this scheme, "I" and "J" are given the same code.)

Julius Caesar, the first century BC Roman statesman, used at least two ciphering systems during the years when he was a general of the Roman armies. These systems are the Caesar Shift and the Caesar Box Codes (we describe both in Chapter 2, and you can try your hand at them in Chapters 7 and 11). After the fall of the Roman Empire in the West (about 476 AD), we know little of the making of codes and ciphers in the West for many centuries.

However, in other parts of the world, cryptography thrived. The rise of Islamic civilization, from the seventh century AD onward, saw the first books written on *cryptanalysis,* that is, the organized effort to *break* codes and ciphers.

In Eastern Asia, the use of *idiograms* (picture writing) in such languages as Chinese made it impractical to use *ciphers* (substitutes for letters). However, real codes were sometimes used. For example, in 11th century AD China, one military code was based on the 30 words of a particular poem. Each word corresponded to a brief message, like "need more bows and arrows." A single word of the poem would be sent as the message from one commander to his superior.

The rebirth of learning during the Renaissance, which continued in the Enlightenment, saw a great increase in the use of codes and ciphers in the Western world. The emergence of the central text of Kabbalah, the Zohar, in about 1300, led many Christian scholars to look into the use of *gematria* to detect secret meanings in sacred writ. The publication of Agrippa's *Three Books of Occult Philosophy* in 1531 did a great deal to spread the use of special alphabets to conceal secret religious writings because Agrippa was the first to publish together in tabular form the magical alphabets called "Celestial," "Malachim" (Hebrew for "angels"), and the enigmatically named "Passing the River." These magical alphabets were republished centuries later in Francis Barrett's popular work, *The Magus* (1801), through which these alphabets became a permanent part of the landscape of esoteric and magical studies. (You can try some of these magical alphabets in Chapters 6 and 8.)

But it is the worlds of politics and military actions that have seen an explosion of activity in the area of secret writing over the last 600 years. The destinies of nations have hung on the making and breaking of codes. For example, the attempt by Mary Queen of Scots to take the British throne from Elizabeth I of England in 1585 collapsed when the cipher used by her conspirators, led by Anthony Babington, was broken by Elizabeth's agents.

As cryptography made and unmade nations in Europe, it did the same in the New World. For example, in the American Revolutionary War, a wide variety of cryptographic techniques (including ciphers, code books, and invisible inks) was used on both sides. The same is true of the use of cryptography during the American War Between the States, or Civil War.

Cryptography and the Great Wars

During the wars of the 20th century, cryptography came to determine the destiny, not just of nations, but of the globe.

We offer you three examples, one from the First World War and two from the Second. Both wars began in Europe, with the entry of the United States following sometime afterward.

The Zimmerman telegram

By early 1917, the First World War had been raging on the continent of Europe for two and a half years, but the U.S. was officially neutral. The question on everyone's mind was whether the U.S. would enter the war, and if so, when. On January 16, 1917, the German Foreign Secretary (equivalent to the American Secretary of State), Arthur Zimmerman, sent a ciphered telegram to the German ambassador to Mexico. The British intelligence services intercepted the telegram, which consisted of hundreds of groups of digits, each group up to 5 digits long ("13042 13401 8501 115" and so forth). The British had captured some German code books that described an earlier version of the cipher and so were able to decode the message.

The Zimmerman telegram described a plot in which the Germans would begin "unrestricted submarine warfare" on February 1. If America entered the war, Germany proposed to help Mexico reconquer territories in Texas, New Mexico, and Arizona from the U.S.! A way was found to leak this telegram to the U.S. government without revealing that the British had broken the German cipher. The telegram's message was printed in American newspapers on March 1, 1917, and the U.S. entered the war just over a month later. The entry of the U.S. decisively tipped the balance of power in the war away from Germany. The deciphering of the Zimmerman telegram thus changed the course of history.

The Enigma code

In the Second World War, German U-boats were destroying a large fraction of the Allied shipping in the Atlantic Ocean. The Germans used a coding machine, code-named the Enigma, which used a collection of cipher wheels and switches to apply a different cipher to *every single letter of a message*. The British applied an immense amount of effort to breaking this code, which they finally did. The breaking of the Enigma code turned the tide of the war in the Atlantic and made the D-Day invasion that much more possible.

The future of cryptography

Beginning in the 1960s, cryptographers used higher mathematics to make more and more complicated ciphers. These ciphers involve the use of enormously long prime numbers to create ciphers of such complexity that they can only be broken, if at all, with immensely powerful computers. We don't use those ciphers in this book. However, if you're interested in cryptography, you should know that this is where a large part of the future of cryptography is headed. If you're still in school and interested in cryptography, work hard at those math courses!

The Navajo code talkers

In the Pacific theatre of the Second World War, the American armed forces used Native American speakers of the Navajo language. The Navajo code talkers used words from the natural world to represent military objects: different types of birds were different types of aircraft, different types of fish were different types of ships, and so on. The Navajo code talkers were used to communicate among different American military units, with great success. After the war, it was revealed that the Japanese had broken several American codes but had made no progress with breaking Navajo. Much of the American success in the Pacific theatre can be attributed to the contribution of the Navajo code talkers.

Uncovering Masonic Codes and Ciphers

Not everyone who uses codes and ciphers is involved in military or political activity. Groups with a spiritual orientation have long used ciphers and codes to conceal their teachings. This isn't so much for fear of their being discovered (although sometimes this has been a concern, when persecution is an issue). Rather, the issue is to keep certain types of spiritual knowledge or teachings from those who aren't ready or aren't qualified to receive them.

The Freemasons (or Masons), a fraternal organization that has been public about its existence since 1717, has long used codes of different sorts. The primary purpose of using codes has been to keep the Masonic ceremonies of initiation secure. These ceremonies are complex and must be performed from memory. Masons put hours of study into the effort to learn their ceremonies. In some areas, Masons possess small books with the text of these ceremonies. To keep the ceremonies confidential even if the books fall into the wrong hands, the books are written in an *initial-letter cipher,* that is, a code in which each word of the text is represented by its initial letter. This code allows someone who already knows the ceremony to use the cipher to practice the ceremony until the person memorizes it to perfection.

In earlier generations, Freemasons sometimes used symbols instead of letters to encipher their ceremonies. Coauthor Mark has in his possession a couple of book lover's treasures, small old ritual books with ceremonies enciphered by symbol, a sort of American hieroglyphic extravaganza. If you come upon any of these books in an old bookstore or yard sale, treasure them — they become rarer every year.

Masons have also made great use of the *Pigpen Cipher,* so called because, to people of an earlier age, its tic-tac-toe-board structure resembled the layout of pigpens. The Pigpen Cipher has many versions and has come to be known as the Freemasons' Cipher. The version in this book isn't "the" correct one because a single correct version doesn't exist. Masons in different areas learned different versions. However, the version we present in Chapter 8 shows the exotic, mysterious character of the cipher, where letters are represented by a few angular symbols and dots.

On the continent of Europe, where Freemasonry developed in ways that were a bit different from English Masonry, there was more of an interest in exotic ciphers. You can find some of those ciphers in Chapter 8, as well. They're elaborate symbolic inventions dating from the 18th and 19th centuries. In that era, all ciphers had to be written out by hand, so it didn't matter that the ciphers used unique symbols that can't easily be represented in computer-readable form.

Enjoy these ciphers as a glimpse into a different age, when the creation of cryptograms was a bit more leisurely than it is today.

Continuing Your Crypto Education

In this section, we include some reading suggestions for those of you who are hooked on codes, cryptograms, and conspiracies!

Consider these additional resources if you seek to solve more puzzles:

✔ *Word Searches For Dummies* by Denise Sutherland (Wiley): This book, by one of the authors of the book you hold in your hands, shows you how to approach word search puzzles of different types and levels of difficulty. The book includes 250 puzzles to solve, with hints and answers.

✔ *The Mammoth Book of Secret Codes and Cryptograms* by Elonka Dunin (Running Press): This book includes a huge collection of codes and ciphers, as well as real-life unsolved codes and undeciphered scripts.

If you want to gain additional knowledge about codes, ciphers, and cryptography, give these books a try:

✔ *Codebreaker: The History of Codes and Ciphers* by Stephen Pinnock (Walker & Company): This brief and lavishly illustrated book may be the best place to go next if you want to dive further into the subject, especially from a historical point of view.

✔ *The Code Book: The Evolution of Secrecy from Mary, Queen of Scots to Quantum Cryptography* by Simon Singh (Doubleday): As the subtitle indicates, the focus in this book is on the last four centuries or so. You can find extensive examples of different ciphers in this fascinating book.

✔ *The Codebreakers: The Story of Secret Writing* by David Kahn (Macmillan): This is the big daddy of all books on cryptography, a highly readable yet comprehensive description of the entire history of the field. It gives a great deal of emphasis to the period of World War II and the Cold War, but it also includes much about codemaking and codebreaking during earlier periods of history.

    ✔ *Kahn on Codes: Secrets of the New Cryptology* by David Kahn (Macmillan): For the true crypto fan, this is a collection of essays, largely focused on the World War II period and thereafter.

If you want more information about codes in the Kabbalah, we suggest *Kabbalah* by Gershom Scholem (Meridian/Penguin). For cryptographers, the chapter on *gematria* is particularly interesting!

If you want information on cryptography and its use in the American Revolutionary War and the Civil War, turn to these texts:

    ✔ *George Washington, Spymaster: How the Americans Outspied the British and Won the Revolutionary War* by Thomas B. Allen (National Geographic): This book for young adults has a great deal about true codes and other secret writing techniques used during the Revolutionary War. For example, the book reproduces the nine-page codebook created by Major Benjamin Tallmadge, who was General Washington's spy chief — and who appears as a character in our first conspiracy story (see Chapter 3).

    ✔ *Washington's Spies: The Story of America's First Spy Ring* by Alexander Rose (Bantam): This groundbreaking history of the subject has a lot to say about ciphers and codes.

    ✔ *Secret Missions of the Civil War: First-Hand Accounts by Men and Women Who Risked Their Lives in Underground Activities for the North and the South* by Philip Van Doren Stern (Bonanza Books): The final chapter of this book includes info on codes and ciphers in the Civil War.

And if you're looking for information about Freemasonry and its ciphers, consider the following:

    ✔ *Freemasons For Dummies* by Christopher Hodapp (Wiley): This book is an excellent introduction to the general subject of Freemasonry. It tells you how Freemasonry operates, what the Masonic "degrees" or rituals of initiation are like, and how to tell the difference between truth and fantasy in the many stories you can read about Freemasonry in literature and on the Internet.

✔ *Freemasonry: An Introduction,* by Mark Koltko-Rivera (LVX Publishing): This book, by one of the authors of the book you hold in your hands, describes the ideals and values of Freemasonry, its relationship to ancient systems of initiation, and why men choose to become Freemasons in the first place.

✔ *Scottish Rite Ritual Monitor and Guide,* 2nd Edition, by Arturo de Hoyos (Washington, DC: The Supreme Council of the Scottish Rite, 33°, Southern Jurisdiction): If you're a real fan of Masonic ciphers, this book gives you traditional Scottish Rite alphabets and ciphers, including the *Cypher of the Rose Croix* devised by Albert Pike, and several other cryptographic treats. (This is the source of the 19th century Masonic Ciphers we use in this book.) For more info, check out www.scottishrite.org.

✔ *Committed to the Flames: The History and Rituals of a Secret Masonic Rite* by Arturo de Hoyos and S. Brent Morris (Lewis Masonic): This book describes the effort that successfully deciphered a custom Masonic Cipher that resisted all efforts to break it for over a century. The result revealed a secret set of ceremonies that were used by a small Masonic group in New York.

Chapter 2

Simplifying Codes and Cryptograms

*P*eople have been hiding their messages from prying eyes for millennia. Their methods became more complex as time went on, and encryption is still a vital part of modern life. You can read more about the history of codes and ciphers in Chapter 1.

Ingenious people have devised many ciphers over the years, and no doubt there are more ciphers to come! In this book we include several different types of ciphers and several variations on these types. We hope you enjoy this selection!

The ciphers in this book are

- ✔ Cryptograms with Letter Substitutions (Chapter 4)
- ✔ Cryptograms with Number Substitutions (Chapter 5)
- ✔ Cryptograms with Symbol Substitutions (Chapter 6)
- ✔ Caesar / Shift Ciphers (Chapter 7)
- ✔ Masonic Ciphers (Chapter 8)
- ✔ Rail Fence Ciphers (Chapter 9)
- ✔ Keyboard Ciphers (Chapter 10)
- ✔ Assorted Ciphers (Chapter 11)
- ✔ Anagrams and Other Cryptic Riddles (Chapter 12)
- ✔ Double Level Puzzles (Chapter 13)

We also include a very handy collection of hints in Chapter 14. If you're really stuck, look there before giving in to the allure of the answers (Chapter 15).

This book is a bit unusual, too, because in Chapter 3 we present you with three conspiracy stories, set in different times in American history. These stories have been heavily censored by the government — your task is to decipher the puzzles in the book in order to gain access to these secret files. All the puzzles are numbered carefully so you can easily see which puzzle goes where.

If you prefer to do puzzles for fun without worrying about solving the conspiracy stories, that's perfectly fine too, of course! We include a lot of cryptograms that aren't related to the Chapter 3 stories, and the story-related ciphers are enjoyable to crack even if you don't solve the conspiracy.

Considering Cryptography Terms

Although they're often used to mean the same thing, strictly speaking a code is quite different from a cipher. Consider these definitions:

- ✔ A *code* **is a whole new language.** Entire words are encoded by a number, symbol, or another word. For example, CONSPIRACY may be encoded as *32, u,* or *falcon.* A code book is required to crack a code, and it basically functions as a dictionary of the code's language.

  Codes are very hard to crack, but the need for code books is their weakness — if a code book falls into the wrong hands, your code is useless and your plans are discovered!

- ✔ A *cipher* **is a way of rearranging or replacing the letters in a message.** In substitution ciphers, each letter of the alphabet (and sometimes the numbers and punctuation) are replaced by another letter, number, or symbol. The letter *D* may be enciphered as *R, 9,* or ✳, for example.

  Ciphers can be easier to crack than a code, but they're also more secure. You can often memorize the key to a cipher, so you don't need written instructions. That eliminates the major security failing of codes. Ciphers

> are also easy to change regularly, which is an important
> strategy if you really rely on encryption (as opposed to
> those of us who just enjoy the mental workout for fun).

Although we use the words *code, decode,* and *encode* in this
book interchangeably with *cipher, decipher,* and *encipher,* rest
assured that all the puzzles in this book are *ciphers.*

Before you dive into the puzzles, familiarize yourself with a
few terms for this book:

- ✔ *Plaintext* is the secret message that you need to discover;
  the English is written out *plain* so anyone can read it.
  You typically see plaintext written in lowercase letters,
  especially within encryption keys.

- ✔ *Ciphertext* is the encrypted message. You usually see
  ciphertext written in UPPERCASE letters.

- ✔ A *keyword* is a vital, or key, word or phrase that's used to
  further complicate a cipher and helps to decode a cipher.

- ✔ In a *substitution cipher,* the letters of the alphabet are substituted with other letters, numbers, or symbols.

- ✔ In a *transposition cipher,* the letters of the message are
  rearranged into a new order according to a set pattern
  instead of being changed into other symbols.

- ✔ A *pattern word* is any word with repeated letters and is
  invaluable for cracking ciphers. PEOPLE and THAT are
  two pattern words, having the pattern 1 2 - 1 - 2, and
  1 -- 1, respectively. 1 and 2 refer to the repeating code
  letters in an encrypted word.

Figure 2-1 gives you an example of plaintext (lowercase) and
ciphertext (uppercase) encryption, with a keyword of NEW
YORK. The rest of the alphabet, minus the letters in NEW
YORK, is filled in after the keyword.

```
a b c d e f g h i j k l m n o p q r s t u v w x y z
N E W Y O R K A B C D F G H I J L M P Q S T U V X Z
```
Figure 2-1: An example of plaintext and ciphertext encryption.

In this particular cipher, the message LEAVE TOWN would be
enciphered as FONTO QIUH.

Solving the Ciphers in This Book

In this section we take you through each puzzle type in this book and give you a few handy strategies for solving them.

Cryptograms with Letter, Number, and Symbol Substitutions

In any substitution cipher, each letter of the alphabet is substituted for other symbols. These symbols may be letters, numbers, or symbols.

You can work with other complex variations (in which one message has multiple encodings, for example), but in this book we concentrate on simple substitution ciphers. Chapter 4 contains letter substitutions, Chapter 5 has number substitutions, and Chapter 6 has symbol substitution ciphers.

When approaching a substitution cipher, here are some basics to keep in mind:

- ✔ Use a pencil and eraser!

- ✔ Look for single-letter words. They're *almost* always *A* or *I*.

- ✔ Count how many times each symbol appears in the cipher, and write it down. The most frequent letter is likely to be *E* — but *T, O,* and *A* are also good contenders.

- ✔ A letter is never encoded as itself: *D = D* for example. (Caesar Ciphers with keywords are a rare exception to this rule.)

- ✔ Two-letter words almost always have one vowel and one consonant.

- ✔ Look for the two most common three-letter words: AND and THE.

- ✔ Look for *pattern words,* especially THAT, which is the most common four-letter word. (See the previous section for a definition of *pattern words.*)

- ✔ Pencil in your guesses, and look for clashing letter combinations (for example, you can be sure that *KVC* isn't the start of any English word).

✔ After writing a decrypted letter above its cipher, read through the whole encrypted message and write that letter wherever the cipher letter appears in the message. For example, if you find that *K = A,* go through the ciphertext and write an *A* over every *K.*

Seeing all the instances of one letter in a ciphertext is surprisingly difficult to do. That's probably because you read by seeing the whole *shape* of a word; most people don't read by looking at each individual letter in succession. So read through the ciphertext several times, and be prepared to keep finding instances popping out at you!

For more hints on how to crack substitution ciphers, read the later section about letter frequency analysis.

Caesar / Shift Ciphers

A Caesar / Shift Cipher was widely used by the Roman emperor Julius Caesar. Chapter 7 is the place to go for these puzzles.

With a Caesar / Shift Cipher, all the letters in the alphabet are shifted by a set amount (such as +5, or –2). To create a Caesar / Shift Cipher, you write the cipher alphabet in order under the plain alphabet, wrapping it around from *Z* to *A* until all letters are assigned. Figure 2-2 shows you an example of a Caesar / Shift Cipher.

```
abcdefghijklmnopqrstuvwxyz
EFGHIJKLMNOPQRSTUVWXYZABCD


Meet me at the big oak
QIIX QI EX XLI FMK SEO
```

Figure 2-2: An example of a Caesar / Shift Cipher with a +4 shift.

Caesar / Shift Ciphers often use a *keyword*. In this case, you write a word at the start of the cipher, and then you write the remainder of the alphabet in order. Figure 2-3 shows you an example; the keyword here is SPHINX.

```
a b c d e f g h i j k l m n o p q r s t u v w x y z
S P H I N X A B C D E F G J K L M O Q R T U V W Y Z
```

```
Bring  Susan  to  the  cafe
POCJA  QTQSJ  RK  RBN  HSXN
```
Figure 2-3: A Caesar / Shift Cipher with SPHINX as the keyword.

If the keyword has repeating letters, only the first instance of each letter is used (so LONDON TOWN would be written as LONDTW).

A Caesar / Shift Cipher with a keyword often ends up coding letters as themselves by the end of the alphabet, so it's common for $X = X$, $Y = Y$, and $Z = Z$, unless these letters appear in the keyword. This coding is an unusual feature of these particular ciphers.

Masonic Ciphers

Chapter 8 contains a bevy of ciphers used by Freemasons over the centuries. One is the Masonic Cipher, which is also known as the Pigpen Cipher (because the grid looks like a pigpen — you be the judge!). We also present you with the *Cypher of the Rose Croix,* and other special substitution ciphers made with Masonic symbols and alphabets, such as Malachim and Celestial.

The Masonic Cipher is a variety of substitution cipher — each letter is substituted by a symbol. If you use this cipher to send and receive messages, you can create the code symbols in a way that makes it very easy to remember how to construct and re-create the key. See Figure 2-4 for an example of a Masonic Cipher.

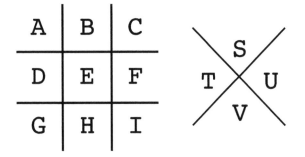

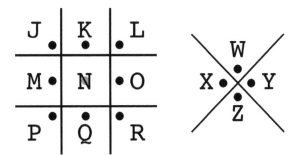

```
FLEE THE STATE,
DESTROY ALL EVIDENCE
```

```
⌐Ŀ□□  >∩□  V>⌐⌐>□ ,
⊐□V>ᖴᘓ<  ⌐Ŀ⌐  □∧⌐⊐□◖L□
```

Figure 2-4: An example of the Masonic Cipher.

You can also use keywords within a Masonic Cipher to further complicate matters. In this format, pairs of letters are written into each location, as in Figure 2-5. First write the keyword (in this case, LODGE) and then write the remainder of the alphabet into the grids in letter pairs. The second letter in each pair is enciphered with a dot.

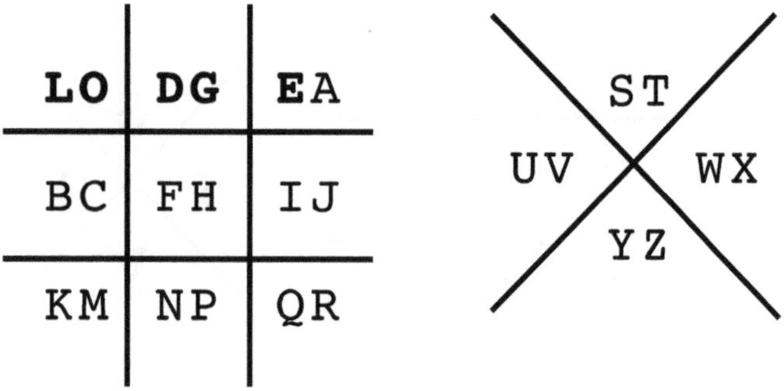

LO	DG	EA
BC	FH	IJ
KM	NP	QR

The treasure is in the dog house

Figure 2-5: A Masonic Cipher with the keyword LODGE.

Some 19th century Masons used *magical writing systems,* such as Celestial and Malachim. These symbol systems are based on Hebrew, and they generally represent sounds rather than fixed letters. Figure 2-6 includes a table of the English letters and sounds that most closely correspond to the Malachim symbols.

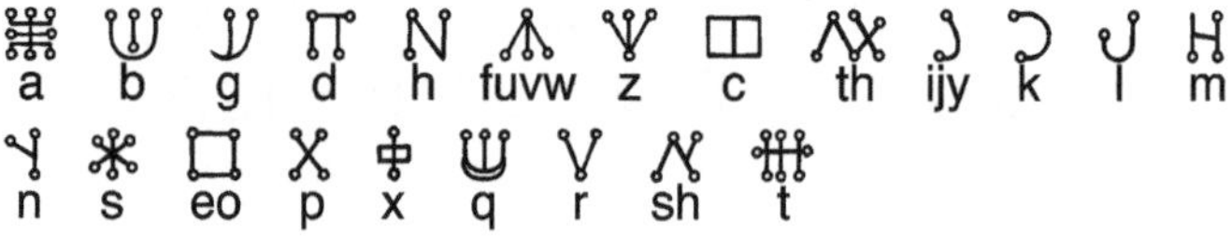

Figure 2-6: The phonetic Malachim alphabet.

To solve a Malachim or other special font Masonic Cipher, you occasionally have to choose between two or more sounds for a single symbol. Generally the two letters are closely related in pronunciation, such as v and w. The encryption is a phonetic encryption rather than a straight symbol substitution. (The Malachim letter we mark as x should technically be ts or tz. We use x for the sake of utility — in English you simply need x more than tz.)

Rail Fence Ciphers

A Rail Fence Cipher is a transposition cipher. The letters in the message aren't changed, but their positions are altered. Unless you know the encryption method, these ciphers can be very difficult to crack. You can find them in Chapter 9.

To decipher these codes, you need to know the number of rails. With a two-rail cipher, you simply divide your ciphertext into halves, and then write the second half underneath the first half, slightly offset. Then you can read off the plaintext by alternating between the top and bottom rails of your letter fence. Figure 2-7 shows you an example of a two-rail cipher.

For ciphers with more than two rails, the process is more complicated because you have to figure out how many letters to have in each rail to crack the code. The number of "points" of the zigzag in the top row is the most important thing to figure out.

To solve these ciphers, try drawing a zigzag onto a lined piece of paper with a colored pencil or highlighter pen. Then write the ciphertext from left to right and top to bottom in order, following the zigzag path. The horizontal lines on your page will help you keep everything lined up (so if you aren't using lined paper, draw some horizontal lines!). These lines are the rails.

A three-rail cipher is drawn over three lines, a four-rail cipher is drawn over four lines, and so on. Figure 2-7 shows two examples of Rail Fence Ciphers.

If a message has too few letters to fit into the chosen rail pattern (a fairly common occurrence) dummy letters are added to the end of the message to pad it out. So don't be put off if an X or other random letter or two appears at the end of your message.

Draw the zigzag so the last section is just coming up to — but stops just *short* of — another point. Refer to the way the zigzags are drawn in Figure 2-7.

2 rails SATLN LHADW TRPAA PATAN

SATLN LHADW | TRPAA PATAN

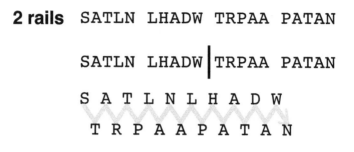

3 rails STNHD TRPAA PATAN ALLAW

Figure 2-7: Two- and three-rail Fence Ciphers of the message
START PLAN ALPHA AT DAWN.

The following sets of steps show you the way to crack the bigger, and harder, Rail Fence Ciphers.

For a three-rail cipher:

1. Count the letters in the cipher.
2. Divide the letters into four equal parts.
3. Draw your zigzag with a number of points on the top rail equal to ¼ of the total letters.
4. Place your letters across the grid. One quarter go on the top rail, half fit on the middle rail, and the final quarter fit along the bottom rail.

For a four-rail cipher:

1. Count the letters in the cipher.
2. Divide the letters into six equal parts.

3. **Draw your zigzag with a number of points on the top rail equal to ⅙ of the total letters.**

4. **Place your letters across the grid.** One sixth go on the top rail, a third fit on the second rail, the next third fit on the third rail, and the final sixth fit along the bottom rail.

For a five-rail cipher:

1. **Count the letters in the cipher.**

2. **Divide the letters into eight equal parts.**

3. **Draw your zigzag with a number of points on the top rail equal to ⅛ of the total letters.**

4. **Place your letters across the grid.** One eighth go on the top rail; a quarter fit on each of the second, third, and fourth rails; and the final eighth fit along the bottom rail.

The Rail Fence Ciphers in this book have all been designed to fit neatly into the two-, three-, four- and five-rail patterns, with no pesky extra letters. If you try to apply this solving method on Rail Fence Ciphers elsewhere, you may be out by one. You can normally sort it out by trial and error.

Rail Fence Ciphers sometimes include the spaces between words as blank characters in the cipher. We don't have this variety in this book, but you may come across them elsewhere.

Keyboard Ciphers

Keyboard Ciphers are created with some of our favorite bits of technology — our cellphones and computer keyboards! These puzzles are in Chapter 10.

Text Message Ciphers

Text Message (or SMS) Ciphers make use of your phone. Multiple letters occupy each number key on a phone; the 2 key has the letters *ABC* written on it, for example.

These letters have long been used to create memorable phone numbers. You know the sort of thing: "Call 1-800-MORE-COFFEE *now* for *more coffee!*" This is a simple letter-to-number encryption of the phone number 1-800-6673-263333.

In this book, however, we go in the opposite direction, from number to letter.

You're probably already all too familiar with using your cellphone keypad to type text messages. Most phones use *predictive text* now, in which the phone's software guesses at what you mean when you input a certain number sequence. This guess is based on common words used in English.

For example, to type HOME, you press 4663. However, this combination of number keys also encodes the words GOOD, GONE, HOOD, HOOF, and several less-common words.

The fiendish Text Message Ciphers in this book take advantage of this ambiguity. They're simply a collection of numbers, made to type a secret message. Your job is to figure out what the intended words are!

Look for common patterns, such as 843 (THE), 263 (AND), and 8438 (THAT) within these ciphers.

Because each number can represent three or four different letters (unlike in a substitution cipher, where each symbol represents a single letter), you have to try several letter options for each word.

The context of the message helps you decipher these puzzles. For example, with the message 7323 8447 2665, the first two words are pretty easy to pin down: READ THIS. However, 2665 is more problematic; it can be COOL, COOK, or BOOK. Obviously, the first two words indicate that the correct message is READ THIS BOOK, because READ THIS COOL doesn't make sense. (Or *does* it? Maybe we can start a new fad here!)

Use your cellphone to help crack these codes. Start a new text message (that you won't send to anyone), and type in the numbers to see which words are options.

Be careful, though — the phone's dictionary is very limited. Foreign words, unusual words, and proper nouns generally aren't included.

Typewriter Ciphers

Humans have a long history of using "code machines" to physically create a cipher. Strips of paper wrapped around rods (*scytales*) and pivoting cardboard circles for offsetting alphabets are just a couple of these devices, and you can go right up to the incredibly complex Enigma machine used during World War II, not to mention modern computer encryption methods.

In this book, some ciphers use a typewriter or computer keyboard as the method of encryption. The concept is quite simple — you simply shift which key you press by a set movement.

For example, you may type your message by using the keys *one up and to the left* of your intended letters. Or perhaps you move *one key down and to the right.* Check out Figure 2-8 for examples of these Typewriter Ciphers.

Punctuation is often found as one of the encrypted characters in these ciphers, and uppercase letters can be encoded differently from lowercase letters. So if you see a message that has an odd mix of numbers, letters, and punctuation, you may be looking at a keyboard code.

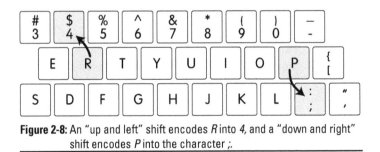

Figure 2-8: An "up and left" shift encodes *R* into *4,* and a "down and right" shift encodes *P* into the character *;.*

Assorted Ciphers

You can find a ton of different codes and ciphers out in the world; we only scratch the surface in this book! Chapter 11 is our chance to broaden the field and show you a range of codes and ciphers that aren't anywhere else in the book. We include the Atbash Cipher, Caesar Box Cipher, Twisted Path Box Cipher, Newspaper Codes, and a few Columnar Transpositions (described in the later section on Double Level Puzzles).

Atbash Ciphers

The Atbash Cipher is one of the oldest and simplest ciphers. It was originally used with the Hebrew alphabet. You simply wrap the alphabet around on itself, so A = Z and Z = A, B = Y and Y = B, and so on. Figure 2-9 shows you what it looks like.

ABCDEFGHIJKLM
ZYXWVUTSRQPON

Figure 2-9: Atbash Ciphers wrap the alphabet around on itself.

Caesar Box Ciphers

The Caesar Box Cipher is another cipher used by Julius Caesar. It's a *transcription cipher* rather than a substitution cipher, which means the letters in the message aren't altered, but their positions are muddled up.

The Caesar Box Cipher works best for messages with a square number of letters (for example, 3 x 3 = 9, 4 x 4 = 16, 5 x 5 = 25, and so on). You can add null letters to the end of a message to pad it to the correct length, or the grid can be a rectangle rather than a square.

The plaintext is written down the columns of the grid, and then read off in rows. This forms the ciphertext. Figure 2-10 shows the message JENNY GOT THE EMAIL.

Then the letter groups are read off in rows, resulting in an encoded message of JYTM EGHA NOEI NTEL.

To crack a Caesar Box Cipher, first figure out the number of letters.

Box ciphers are sometimes presented with letters in groups, which is also a hint as to the grid size. For example, if you see seven groups of seven letters in the ciphertext, you need to draw up a 7 x 7 grid.

J	Y	T	M
E	G	H	A
N	O	E	I
N	T	E	L

Figure 2-10: A Caesar Box Cipher with a 4 x 4 grid.

If the letters haven't been presented in groups, you may need to count them to get the total.

If you end up with 25 letters, draw up a 5 x 5 box. Write the cipher in, row by row, and then read down the columns to discover the message.

Some box ciphers are laid out in rectangles, so if you have 24 letters, for example, you may be looking at a 6 x 4 grid.

Twisted Path Ciphers

Twisted Path Ciphers are transcription ciphers that are a variation on the Caesar Box Ciphers. Instead of reading off the message in columns from top to bottom, the message is written in a path inside the box. The path may be a spiral (clockwise or counterclockwise), or up and down the columns, or in a reverse order. Figure 2-11 shows you a few examples. Note how each cipher reads quite differently, although they all encode the same message.

Newspaper Codes

In distant days in England, sending a letter was quite expensive, but posting a newspaper was free! Clever people soon figured out a way to send news to friends and family, free of charge. They used a pin to poke a tiny hole above or below letters on a newspaper page. By holding the newspaper up to the light, it was easy to see the pin-pricked letters and read the hidden message.

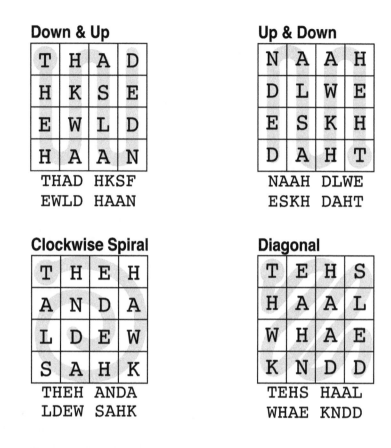

Down & Up

T	H	A	D
H	K	S	E
E	W	L	D
H	A	A	N

THAD HKSF
EWLD HAAN

Up & Down

N	A	A	H
D	L	W	E
E	S	K	H
D	A	H	T

NAAH DLWE
ESKH DAHT

Clockwise Spiral

T	H	E	H
A	N	D	A
L	D	E	W
S	A	H	K

THEH ANDA
LDEW SAHK

Diagonal

T	E	H	S
H	A	A	L
W	H	A	E
K	N	D	D

TEHS HAAL
WHAE KNDD

Figure 2-11: Some Twisted Path Ciphers, all encrypting the 16-letter message THE HAWK HAS LANDED.

In Chapters 11 and 13, we present a few of this type of letter-marking code, in which tiny dots are added to mark the letters. Detect the dots and write down the letters to reveal all!

Anagrams and other cryptic riddles

Anagrams, cryptic clues, and riddles have been around as long as cryptology. Each is a great way of hiding a few words. People even use anagrams of their names to create new personas and pseudonyms. In Chapter 12, we present you with a delectable assortment to try. And who knows, maybe you'll venture into the world of cryptic crosswords and enjoy it!

Anagrams

Anagrams simply rearrange the letters of a word, or words, to create new words. Short words are generally easy to decipher (TEACH = CHEAT), but long anagrams can be challenging to figure out because of the many possible solutions. THE MORSE CODE turns very nicely into HERE COME DOTS, but it could also be SMOOTH DECREE, or one of several *hundred* other combinations.

Some of the anagrams in this book are just jumbled collections of letters, and others spell out new words — we know you can spot which is which!

When you're faced with an unruly collection of letters, try some of the following tricks to help you tame them:

- ✔ Write the anagram backward or in a circle. The idea is to mix up the letters even more to help break up the strong patterns you're seeing in the starting words.

- ✔ Divide the letters into vowels and consonants. This tip is particularly helpful for long anagrams.

- ✔ Write the scrambled letters in alphabetical order.

- ✔ Look for common patterns that you can make with the group of letters you have: SH, CH, TH, HE, AN, RE, IE, LL, EE, and so on.

In this book, we make sure that the message's letter count pattern is given in the anagram. So if the words in the final message are PICK UP ANDREWS AT TWO, the anagram has the numbers (4, 2, 7, 2, 3) at the end.

Cryptic Clues

We include a few of the simpler varieties of Cryptic Clues in this book. For a more complete discussion of these tricky puzzles, coauthor Denise recommends *Cryptic Crosswords & How to Solve Them* by Fred Piscop (Sterling) and *Solving Cryptic Crosswords* by B. J. Holmes (A & C Black).

The basic construction of any cryptic clue is that it must contain the *base clue* (which is a straight definition for the answer, like a regular crossword clue) as well as some sort of *word play*. The base clue almost always occurs either at the start or end of the clue (not in the middle).

A well-constructed cryptic clue is self-checking — when you get it, you get confirmation and a wonderful "ah-ha!" moment.

Anagrams

Anagrams are a popular feature in cryptic clues. The letters from a word in the clue are jumbled up to reveal the answer.

Here's an example:

Confused tale for a duck (4)

In this clue, *confused* is an *anagram indicator*. It tells you that some letters in the clue need to be "confused" or muddled up to find the answer. You'll come across tons of anagram indicators, but some of the main ones include the following:

- Agitated
- Badly
- Broken
- Confused
- Cooked
- Damaged
- In pieces
- Mangled
- Mistaken
- Muddled
- Shaken
- Silly
- Stirred
- Twisted
- Unruly
- Upset

The letter count is also very helpful. You can see that the answer to this clue has four letters. Generally, this means you can search through the clue for a four-letter word (or a few words that exactly add up to four letters) that can be jumbled to give the answer.

This example includes a few options: TALE, FOR + A, and DUCK. Jumbling the letters of DUCK doesn't bring any joy, nor does FOR with A. TALE, however, can be rearranged to TEAL — which is a type of duck.

The clue can be read as the following instruction: "If you mix up the letters from the word TALE, you get the name of a duck, which has four letters."

Double Definitions

Double Definition clues may look very confusing, but they're simply two definitions for the same word, strung together.

Here's an example:

> **Gaze at the timepiece (5)**

These clues become clearer if you mentally add a comma between the two definitions:

> **Gaze at, the timepiece (5) = WATCH**

Hidden Words

Hidden Words are words that are literally hidden within a clue. Here's an example:

> **Wasps almost carry a sacred song (5)**

The word *carry* is an *indicator,* giving you a hint to what sort of cryptic clue this is. Hidden Word clues are indicated by words like *carry, hold, hidden, part of, in, found in*, and so on. In this case, *carry* means the answer is *carried* within the letters of *Wasps almost.*

> **Wasps almost carry a sacred song (5) = PSALM**

Here's another one to try:

> **Glimpse a gleaming hidden raptor (5)**

With Hidden Word clues, you know the number of letters (five in this case), so you can simply move through the sequence of letters in the clue, looking for the group of five consecutive letters that spell out the answer. Did you find it? Of course you did. EAGLE.

Double Level Puzzles

The Double Level Puzzles in Chapter 13 are the hardest in the book, and each puzzle consists of two ciphers. The first cipher produces a keyword. Then you use this keyword to unlock the second cipher. Each puzzle in this chapter has individual instructions with it because each has some particular quirks.

Keywords

The keywords in Double Level Puzzles are used in different ways. They may reveal which path to take in a Twisted Path Box Cipher, or how many rails to use in a Rail Fence Cipher.

Sometimes a keyword can encode a number sequence (as in a Columnar Transposition Cipher, which we feature in Chapter 13). All you need to do is find the alphabetical order of the letters in your keyword, and then use that order to generate a number sequence.

For example, if the keyword is BRAZIL, it equates to 251634. *A* comes first in this set of letters alphabetically, *B* is second, *I* comes next in the alphabet, so it's third. *L* and *R* come next, and finally *Z* is in sixth place. The alphabetical position of each letter is written above the word; see Figure 2-12 for an example.

```
2  5  1  6  3  4
B  R  A  Z  I  L
```

Figure 2-12: The keyword and its numerical counterpart.

You then use this sequence (251634) to put columns of encrypted text in the correct order. (Read on to discover everything else you need to know to solve Columnar Transposition Ciphers!)

Columnar Transposition Ciphers

It's rumored that a Columnar Transportation Cipher is featured on the *Krytpos* sculpture by James Sanborn, which stands in front of the CIA headquarters in Langley, Virginia. These ciphers are similar to box ciphers, but they're much more complicated transposition ciphers because the columns of letters are mixed up!

You need to know the order of the columns in order to crack these ciphers. This is where a keyword comes in, with the alphabetic rank of its letters determining the number sequence (see the previous section on keywords for more info).

Don't include any repeated letters in your keyword.

The alphabetic order of the letters in the keyword determines the order of the columns in the cipher, and the number of columns too. In the example here, WAGON gives you five columns, one for each letter, and a number sequence of 51243.

Count the number of letters in the cipher, and divide that count by the number of keyword letters to get the number of rows. In the example in Figure 2-13, there are 20 letters, divided by 5 (the number of letters in WAGON), which gives you 4 rows of letters.

Null letters, like X, J, Z, and Q, often fill any spaces left at the bottom of the grid.

Now you're ready to start writing the cipher in columns. Number the columns in order (1, 2, 3, 4, 5 in this example), and write the letters of the cipher *down the columns,* one after the other. Follow the path of the arrow for the first grid in Figure 2-13.

Keyword: **51243**
          WAGON

The cipher :
GZAAE USPTE SDNRE EAAHC

First grid   Second grid

1	2	3	4	5
G	E	T	N	A
Z	U	E	R	A
A	S	S	E	H
A	P	D	E	C

5	1	2	4	3
A	G	E	N	T
A	Z	U	R	E
H	A	S	E	S
C	A	P	E	D

Agent Azure has escaped

Figure 2-13: A short Columnar Transposition Cipher.

If you're right-handed, write this first grid of the cipher letters on the left side of your paper. If you're left-handed, write this first grid of the cipher on the right side of your paper. Trust us, it makes it easier.

Now, you've done all this work — and the message still doesn't make sense! But don't give up — you're very close now. Here's where the keyword comes into its own.

Draw a second grid with the same number of columns, and this time write the keyword's number sequence above the columns. That sequence was 51243 in our example.

Now transcribe the columns from your *first* grid into the *second* grid, writing them in the order dictated by the keyword. So the first column, numbered 1 from the first grid gets put into the column numbered 1 in the second grid, which happens to be in the *second* position in this instance.

You can now read the message, starting at the top left corner, reading across the rows (following the path of the arrow on the second grid in Figure 2-13). You just need to add spaces between the words, but you've come this far, so that part will be a cinch! Ignore any null letters that were added to the end of the message (unless *they're* a special code from your partner in crime, too!).

Looking at Letter Frequency Analysis

Letter frequency analysis is the way to crack substitution ciphers. It means pretty much what it says: You break down a cipher into its components and analyze how often each one occurs. With an understanding of the letter frequencies that occur in English, you can get a handle on cracking the cipher.

When you use letter frequency analysis to crack a code, you simply count how many times each symbol appears in a section of encoded text. If it's English, you can be fairly certain that the four most commonly occurring symbols will be *E, T, O,* and *A. E* is almost always the most frequently used letter.

We can't give you a definitive list of the frequency of letters in English (or any language) because it changes depending on which texts have been analyzed. We chose one for you, but if you're interested in finding out more, check online or in a cryptography book.

Letter frequency lists read from left to right, from the most frequently used letters to the least.

We broke this list into five letter groups (and six at the end) just to make it a bit easier for you to read.

ETAON RISHD LFCMU GYPWB VKXJQZ

Short ciphertexts with fewer than 100 characters may not fit well with the standard letter-frequency patterns. The frequencies can still help you make educated guesses, though. And ciphers of less than 20 letters may have more than one solution!

Letter and word patterns

If you keep the following pointers in mind, you'll be well on your way to becoming an expert cryptographer!

✔ The 12 most common letters at the beginning of words in English are TAI SOW CMB PHD.

This doesn't mean that more words in the dictionary start with *T* than all the others. Instead, it refers to how often words starting with *T* are seen *in a piece of writing.* The prize position of *T* is linked to how often words like THE, THAT, THIS, THAN, THERE, and so on are used in writing.

✔ The 12 most common ending letters in English are EST NDR YOL AFG.

✔ *Q* is always followed by *U.*

✔ If you have a vowel, the consonant that most often follows it is *N:* AN, EN, IN, ON, UN — they're all popular!

✔ The most common three-letter words in English are AND and THE (see, each appears twice in this sentence!).

✔ The most common four-letter word in English is THAT.

✔ The most frequently seen double letters in English are LL, followed by EE, SS, OO, TT, FF, RR, NN, PP, and CC.

✔ Two-letter words always have at least one vowel, and are *almost* always one consonant and one vowel.

✔ Letters that appear fairly evenly throughout a ciphertext are more likely to be vowels.

✔ Forty percent of any English message is vowels, give or take just 1 percent either way.

✔ Letters that appear less often and are linked with a few repeating characters are more likely to be consonants. For example, *K* appears after *C, L, N, R,* and *S,* and the vowels, but rarely with other letters.

If you're interested in discovering a bigger list of letter frequencies, common letter patterns, and further discussion on this fascinating topic, check out *Word Searches For Dummies* by Denise Sutherland (Wiley).

Pattern words

Pattern words are a crucial part of cracking any cipher. They're simply any word that has repeated letters in it (not just double letters, although those are good, too). The pattern these repeated letters create makes it possible to hunt for the words in an encrypted text.

THAT is the most common pattern word. Any cipher word that's in the pattern 1 - - 1 is almost definitely THAT (see, the T appears twice).

Check out dictionaries of pattern words (*The Cryptogram Dictionary* by Lloyd MacCallum is one you may like). These useful books can tell you all the words that fit the 1 2 2 1 - pattern, for example (ASSAY, DEEDS, KOOKY, TEETH, and TOOTH, just in case you were wondering). The numbers represent the repeating letters.

With practice you'll pick up some of the more common pattern words, like PEOPLE (1 2 - 1 - 2), SELLS (1 - 2 2 1), ELEVEN (1 - 1 - 1 -), and ILLEGALLY (- 1 1 --- 1 1 -).

Adding some space

In particularly difficult ciphertexts, the spaces between words are removed. Would we be that mean? Yes, yes we would . . . but we also give you a clever trick to help you crack this particular problem.

The letter *H* often occurs *before E* (THE, THEN, THERE, THEY, and so on) but very rarely *after E.*

Start by using a letter frequency analysis of your ciphertext to pinpoint the code letter for *E* (it's *probably* the most common letter).

Then look at the ciphertext for which letters appear *before* and *after* the encrypted *E.* The one that almost always appears before the encrypted *E,* and not often after it, is probably the letter *H.*

Now, as long as the secret message doesn't talk a lot about how to behave on behalf of bareheaded racehorses who somehow have preheated beehives, you'll be fine.

It's all Greek to me!

Some ciphers use straight substitutions with established alphabets, such as Cyrillic, Greek, or Korean. So it's not written in a particular language, and you don't need a language class — you just use the symbols and their rough equivalents in English. In this book we use Greek.

The Greek code letters in this book do *not* necessarily correspond with their actual English equivalents. We just use them as cipher symbols.

The world uses many notation systems to communicate: shorthand, semaphore, Braille, maritime signal flags, Morse code, and musical notation are just a few examples. In this book we use Morse code, that darling of the radio waves.

Figure 2-14 lists the basic lowercase Greek and Morse code alphabets. You can find these encryptions in Chapters 6 and 13.

α	β	χ	δ	ε	φ	γ	η	ι	φ	κ	λ	μ
a	b	c	d	e	f	g	h	i	j	k	l	m

ν	o	π	θ	ρ	σ	τ	υ	ϖ	ω	ξ	ψ	ζ
n	o	p	q	r	s	t	u	v	w	x	y	z

·—	—···	—·—·	—··	·	··—·	——·	····	··	·———	—·—	·—··	——
a	b	c	d	e	f	g	h	i	j	k	l	m

—·	———	·——·	——·—	·—·	···	—	··—	···—	·——	—··—	—·——	——··
n	o	p	q	r	s	t	u	v	w	x	y	z

Figure 2-14: The Greek and Morse code alphabets.

Part II

Secret Stories, Codes, and Cryptogram Puzzles

The 5th Wave   By Rich Tennant

"Well, Mr. Humphrey, it appears that working on puzzles for hours on end certainly DOES have some side effects."

In this part . . .

You're confronted with three tales of conspiracy, composed by Freemason and writer Mark E. Koltko-Rivera. One conspiracy dates to the days of the Revolutionary War; another takes place over the course of 70 years before and after the Civil War; and the third takes place — well, yesterday, today, and tomorrow. Ah, but important phrases and portions of each story are in code! How will you ever discover the truth of these conspiracies?

By solving the many puzzles we include in this part. The solutions give you the coded pieces of the story to plug into Chapter 3 so you can read our conspiracy stories.

If you're more interested in the puzzles than the stories, you can work through Chapters 4 through 13 for fun, without ever deciphering Chapter 3. Plus you can find plenty of cryptograms in this part that aren't related to the stories at all. No matter what you prefer, this part is filled with enough codes and cryptograms to keep you busy for quite some time!

Chapter 3

Solving Stories

* *

In This Chapter

▶ Diving into an American Revolutionary War conspiracy

▶ Following a Civil War–era conspiracy

▶ Uncovering a modern-day conspiracy

* *

*T*his book contains a wealth of ciphers for you to crack. Some of them are quotations or apt sayings. But most of our messages offer you something more — not just one conspiracy story, but *three!*

We *tried* to write the full stories for you in this chapter, but the government censor discovered the letters and documents, and now large sections of each story are missing and encrypted. Your mission, if you choose to accept it, is to decipher the missing portions from each story and unearth the real story of what happened!

To solve these conspiracy stories, simply find the puzzle number next to each gap, and solve that cipher in Part II to fill in the gap!

If you don't want to follow the stories in this chapter, that's perfectly fine too. You can solve all the ciphers in this book just for the fun of it, without putting them into the story.

The Conspiracy of West Point: 1779–1780

This conspiracy takes place during the days of the American Revolutionary War.

_____(271).

In the spring of 1779, at the height of the American Revolution, an unexpected message is passed to Major John André, who has recently been _____

_____

_____

_____(3).

May 1, 1779

To Major John André, of British Secret Intelligence

Dearest Sir,

_____

_____ (113).

We have known each other as _____ (277) on the field of combat. However, _____

_____

_____

_____ (60).

Please consider this offer and let me know how we might proceed to pursue this opportunity.

Very truly yours,

General Benedict Arnold

Continental Army

_____

_____

_____

_____ (236).

He has to establish _____

_____

_____ (126).

He replies:

May 12, 1779

To General Benedict Arnold, Continental Army

Greetings. Well did you say that your message would come to me as a surprise. You will no doubt pardon my need to

_____

_____

_____ (19).

As you are well aware, _____

_____

_____

_____ (70).

May I ask you to ask her: _____

_____

_____ (208),

when we stood _____

_____

_____ (248)?

Major John André

His Majesty's Army

The _____ (178)
responds to Major André's challenge:

May 23, 1779

To Major John André, His Majesty's Army

My _____ (297)
informs me that _____

_____
_____ (147), at
which you _____

_____
_____
_____ (95).

_____
_____ (199)?

General Benedict Arnold

Continental Army

_____
_____ (112).

May 31, 1779

Dear General Arnold,

_____
_____
_____
_____ (2).

Major John André

His Majesty's Army

Major André seeks authority from his own _____
_____ (275).

June 15, 1779

To General Sir Henry Clinton

Dear General Sir Clinton,

I have recently been contacted by none other than General Benedict Arnold of the Continental Army. _____

_____

_____

_____ (4). For these reasons he _____

_____ (237) and

_____

(177). I seek your authority to _____

_____ (146).

By your leave,

Major John André

His Majesty's Army

By July 1779, General Benedict Arnold is _____

_____

_____

_____ (43).

Arnold dickered with _____

_____

_____ (84). Negotiations are halted in October 1779, when the progress of the war makes communications difficult. In April 1780, General Arnold is

_____

_____(210)

for not _____

_____
_____ (59).
[_____

_____
_____ (239)]

_____
_____ (249). He sends a packet
of information to Major André, with the following cover letter.

June 17, 1780

Dear Major André,

I am pleased to resume our correspondence.

As we long ago discussed, I have pursued a commission as

_____
_____ (179).
Yesterday _____

_____

_____

_____
_____ (82).
I include my specific observations in the attached packet.

I look forward to your judgment of the value of this information, and _____
_____
_____ (114).

General Benedict Arnold

Continental Army

_____

August 3, 1780

Dear Major André,

_____ (209).

_____ (18).

Of course, we must set _____
_____ (145) in advance. Looking
forward to your response, I remain,

Very truly yours,

General Benedict Arnold

Continental Army

August 15, 1780

Dear General Arnold,

_____ (211).

_____ (45).

Major John André

His Majesty's Army

August 30, 1780

Dear Major André,

_____ (180).

_____ (238).

_____

_____

_____

_____ (1).

General Benedict Arnold

Continental Army

_____

_____ (111).

September 7, 1780

General Washington,

_____

_____

_____

_____ (44). Someone high up in
our military is working as _____
_____ (268). However, I have not yet
been able to learn _____
_____ (250).

_____

_____
_____ (46). I shall keep

_____
_____ (148).

Major Benjamin Tallmadge

Commanding, Continental Army Intelligence

September 10, 1780

Major Tallmadge,

_____ (302). _____

_____

_____ (17).

_____

_____ (81).

George Washington, General

Commander-in-Chief

Continental Army

September 12, 1780

General Washington,

_____

_____

_____ (125).

_____

_____ (83),

he _____

_____

_____ (220).

I send this to you with all speed. Please _____

_____ (190).

_____ (188)

September 17, 1780

Major Tallmadge,

_____

_____

_____

_____ (61).

_____ (221).

_____ (93).

This mission is of the highest importance and _____

_____ (305).

George Washington, General

Commander-in-Chief

Continental Army

September 23, 1780

_____ ,

_____

_____

_____ (29). He was carrying on him a _____

_____ (189).

Some of this was in _____ (326). However,

_____

_____

_____

_____

_____ (127).

Major Benjamin Tallmadge

Commanding, Continental Army Intelligence

___

September 24, 1780

General Washington,

_____

_____ (260). _____

_____

_____

_____ (94).

_____

_____(31).

_____ (222).

_____

_____ (200).

_____

_____

_____ (160).

_____

_____ (136)?

Benedict Arnold

formerly General, Continental Army

___

September 28, 1780

Mr. Arnold,

_____

_____

_____ (71).

_____

_____ (105). You did nothing
for your country; you betrayed your country, the country to
which you made an oath of loyalty. _____

_____

_____

_____ (158).

_____

_____

_____

_____ (72).

Finally,

George Washington, General

Commander-in-Chief

Continental Army

September 28, 1780

Major Tallmadge,

_____

_____

_____

_____ (135).

George Washington, General

October 2, 1780

General Washington,

I regret to inform you that _____
_____
_____ (159).
Having been informed that he was in residence _____
_____
_____
_____ (170).
We found out his new location _____
_____
_____
_____ (232).

Major Benjamin Tallmadge

October 10, 1780

General Washington,

Greetings. I have in hand your proposal to _____
_____
_____ (204).
_____ (333).
However, _____
_____ (258).

_____

_____

_____ (104).

Sir Henry Clinton, General

His Majesty's Army

October 17, 1780

General Clinton,

_____

_____ (137).

_____

_____

_____

_____ (230).

_____

_____

_____

_____ (32).

George Washington, General

Continental Army

October 22, 1780

Your Excellency, General Washington,

At the request of Major Benjamin Tallmadge, I make a full report of the events of the evening of September 12, in which I had myself some exceedingly small part.

I serve as _____

_____

_____ (103).

_____ (201); I, in turn, collect no intelligence myself. Thus, _____

_____

_____

_____ (169),

until that night of September 12.

One of Major Tallmadge's agents, _____

_____ (231),

had an urgent message to convey to Major Tallmadge.

_____

_____

_____

_____

_____

_____ (340).

Arriving at my residence, and not finding me there, she made a difficult decision. Sending her boy back home with a kiss and a prayer, _____

_____

_____ (341).

You must understand that _____

_____

_____ (171).

This young woman _____

_____

_____

_____ (261).

_____

_____

_____

_____ (338).

Arriving home hours later and hearing from my housekeeper of your agent's departure, I took off at a gallop to intercept her before the British sentries discovered her message. I was stopped and searched by sentries twice before finding her.

_____

_____

_____

_____

_____ (339).

_____

_____

_____

_____

_____ (342).

I myself then was stopped a third time, and searched at length while she made her departure. _____

_____ (259).

The sentries, sensing some agitation in me, refused me passage; your agent made her journey alone. I had no rest until I learned, four days later, of her safe return to _____ (331).

_____

_____

_____ (343).

Most sincerely yours,

the agent known as

_____ (320)

_____

The following commendation, in cipher, was placed in the
archives of the Continental Congress, passing into the hands of
the Central Intelligence Agency, shortly after its founding in 1947.

_____

_____

_____

_____

_____

_____

_____

_____ (30).

The Conspiracy of the Golden Circle: 1805–1875

This conspiracy begins in the years of Thomas Jefferson's
presidency, not long after the Revolutionary War. It continues
in the decades leading to the Civil War (1860–1864) and sur-
vives into the decade following the war.

January 4, 1805

General James Wilkinson

Governor Appointee, Louisiana Territory

Dear General and Governor Appointee Wilkinson,

It is with great pleasure that I welcome you to the little
arrangement that we have established._____

_____

_____

_____

_____ (8).

_____

_____

_____

_____

_____ (47).

All of this is of no consequence to me, of course. It merely proves to me that you have the _____

_____

_____ (214).

We can make a part of this continent _____ (291).

_____ (183).

I would rather _____

_____

_____ (86),

_____

_____

_____ (115).

What say you? _____

_____

_____

_____ (6).

Sincerely,

Aaron Burr

Vice President of the United States of America

June 17, 1805

The Man of Green

Lexington, Kentucky

Dear Green,

_____
_____
_____
_____ (241).

On the larger question: I agree that our arrangement must become _____
_____
_____
_____ (149).
_____
_____
_____
_____ (62).
_____
_____
_____ (243).

_____
_____ (213).

We carry on.

As always,

Aaron Burr

August 5, 1807

_____ (336):

_____
_____ (96).

_____
_____
_____ (49).

_____
_____
_____ (22).

Burr

Burr was acquitted from his federal _____
_____ (182) because of lack of verifiable evidence.

July 3, 1826

Green:

_____ (215).

_____
_____ (151).

_____
_____
_____ (118).

_____

_____

_____

_____ (252).

You have been my agent, and my friend, for lo these many

years. _____

_____

_____

_____

_____ (85).

My only advice to you: _____

_____ (184).

_____

_____

_____

_____ (7),

and we should not be having this correspondence.

We shall not communicate again.

Burr

_____

Aaron Burr died in 1836.

December 13, 1853

To Burgundy:

_____

_____

_____ (161).

You are instructed to establish a public group, that you

may call (as we discussed earlier) the Knights of the

_____ (281). You will establish

_____

_____ (20),

with the stated agenda of _____

_____

_____ (212).

_____

_____

_____

_____

_____

_____ (129).

As much as possible, _____

_____

_____ (50).

_____

_____ (240).

And now it begins.

Emerald

December 29, 1860

To Burgundy:

_____

_____

_____

_____ (21).

_____

_____

_____ (150).

_____

_____ (181).

The signs of _____

_____ (223)

are unmistakable. I am sure you will have heard by now of

_____

_____ (116).

_____

_____

_____

_____

_____

_____ (5).

_____

_____

_____

_____ (97).

We shall weather this conflict and _____

_____ (285).

Emerald

May 12, 1863

Burgundy:

_____

_____

_____

_____

_____ (48).

_____

_____

_____

_____ (152).

Better to identify more clearly with our own continent.

_____
_____
_____ (193).

_____
_____ (263).

Emerald

July 2, 1864

To Emerald,

It is good to be in touch with you.

_____
_____
_____
_____ (87).
_____
_____
_____
_____
_____
_____ (117).
_____ (242), of course, has us
in a stranglehold. _____
_____
_____ (225).
_____
_____
_____
_____
_____ (88).
_____
_____ (64).

_____
_____
_____ (128) :
_____ (287). _____
_____
_____ (162),
I hope in the near future. In the very worst of circumstances,

_____
_____ (191).

_____
_____ (224)!

_____

_____

_____ (34)

July 4, 1864

Burgundy:

_____
_____
_____ (98).
_____
_____ (74).
_____
_____
_____ (140).

Emerald

September 5, 1864

Dear Emerald,

_____

_____ (251).

_____

_____

_____

_____

_____ (172).

_____

_____ (130).

No doubt this will be our last interchange.

_____ (313).

Jefferson Davis

President

Confederate States of America

_____

October 28, 1864

_____ (309),

_____

_____

_____

_____

_____ (33).

_____
_____
_____ (163).

Emerald

From the Peabody Hotel

Memphis, Tennessee

_____ (233)

My dear Emerald,

_____
_____ (192).

_____
_____
_____ (138).
(_____
_____
_____
_____
_____(63)!
_____
_____
_____ (262))

I am glad that you took the initiative to contact me.

I wish I could make you glad in return, but I cannot.

_____

_____

_____

_____

_____ (139).

However, I present with two insurmountable difficulties
in attempting to aid you. First, I have no means or organization myself that could render any assistance.

_____

_____

_____

_____ (173).

_____

_____

_____

_____

_____

_____

_____

_____ (107).

I enclose a journal with a recent speech of his. _____

_____

_____ (202).

Most sincerely yours,

Jefferson Davis

President, Carolina Life Insurance Company

formerly President, Confederate States of America

To the Honorable Albert Pike, 33rd Degree

Sovereign Grand Commander

The Ancient and Accepted Scottish Rite of Freemasonry

Southern Jurisdiction, U.S.A.

August 31, 1875

Dear Commander Pike,

_____
_____
_____
_____
_____ (75).

_____
_____
_____
_____
_____
_____
_____
_____ (35).

I shall identify myself as I sign myself,

Emerald

September 1, 1875

Mr. Emerald,

In your earlier written communication to me, you assured me that your intentions were most honorable. Given the nature of our discussion on Tuesday night, I have some reason to dispute that.

I can understand why former President Davis had you contact me. _____

_____

_____

_____ (73), mostly outside the domain of the old Union, south of the Mason-Dixon line, and west of the Mississippi. _____

_____

_____

_____

_____ (264).

_____

_____

_____

_____

_____

_____

_____

_____

_____

_____

_____ (174).

_____

_____

_____

_____

_____

_____

_____

_____

_____

_____

_____

_____

_____

_____

_____ (106).

In a few words: No, I shall not help you.

_____

_____

_____

_____

_____ (36).

Most determinedly,

A. Pike

The most prominent sculptress in the Capital communicates with Pike.

September 1, 1875

Albert, my dear one,

I will ask you not to be cross about a temporary deception on my part. _____

_____

_____

_____

_____ (141).
As I came down the stairs, I noticed you enter with a man I had never seen before. Not having anything pressing, I decided to sit on the mezzanine above the tavern floor, off the private office, just gazing upon your face. _____

_____

_____

_____

_____ (76).

Not long after your departure, when your companion stayed at the table, I realized that he was awaiting someone else.

_____

_____

_____

_____

_____

_____ (344).

_____
_____
_____
_____ (345).

Lavinia Ellen "Vinnie" Ream

September 2, 1875

_____

_____
_____
_____
_____
_____ (253).

Burgundy

September 10, 1875

Burgundy,

I am glad that you successfully made it to Arlington, and thence home. I myself took a different route.

_____
_____
_____
_____
_____

_____
_____ (346).

_____
_____
_____ (347).

I'll tell you more at our next scheduled meeting.

Remember: No cause is ever really lost.

Emerald

The Conspiracy of the Organization: 1978–2010

This conspiracy begins in the late 1970s, and continues into the second decade of the 21st century.

28 September 1978

Jade:

_____
_____
_____
_____ (245). _____
_____
_____ (217).

_____
_____
_____
_____ (226).

J. Halligan

October 3, 1978

Special Agent Burton Mannheim

The Federal Bureau of Investigation

The United States Department of Justice

Mr. Mannheim,

_____

_____ (185).

_____

_____

_____

_____

_____ (25),

_____

_____ (91).

_____

_____

_____ (119). _____

_____

_____

_____ (51). _____

_____

_____

_____ (10).

_____

_____

_____ (37).

_____

_____ (194).

_____

_____

_____

_____ (154).

_____

_____

_____

_____

_____

_____ (54).

_____ (317),
and, when it has served its purpose, _____

_____ (186).
Your compliance with these requests will demonstrate to me

_____

_____

_____

_____

_____ (89).

J.

October 27, 1978

Jade:

_____

_____

_____

_____ (131).
Later that day, _____

_____ (53).

I understand that Mannheim is set to receive quite the commendation.

Tan

September 10, 1983

Special Agent Mannheim,

Congratulations on your marriage to the lovely Ms. Loretta Heron. May you have many happy years together.

Now, my young family man, the time has come to consider a change of venue for your career.

You have done a magnificent job at the National Security Division of the FBI. _____

_____ (24),

as well as Justice, within the FBI itself, in Washington and elsewhere. It is time now to hunt for bigger game.

_____ (244)

_____ (65).

Yes, it would be more analysis than fieldwork, but you would be _____

_____

_____ (218).

_____

_____

_____ (195). _____

_____

_____

_____ (120), I would expect that you would do very well in this position. As always, I shall be glad to feed you the information that I can.

Do let me know through our usual channels what you will do about this recommendation. _____

_____

_____ (108).

Jade

January 10, 1992

Mr. Burton Mannheim

Directorate of Intelligence

Central Intelligence Agency

Mr. Mannheim,

I welcome the questions that you sent in your recent communication. _____

_____

_____ (227).

As you have guessed, no, I am not affiliated with any agency of the United States government. Nor am I an agent with a foreign power. _____

_____

_____ (265).

However, as you can guess from the number of foreign agents I have thrown your way over the last dozen years and more, my organization has the interests of America close to heart.

No, Jade is not my real name._____

_____

_____

_____

_____ (12).

I hope that this satisfies your inquiries for the moment. To deal with other matters, I agree heartily that this is the time for you to transfer back to Operations, where some interesting challenges await you.

It is good that you have kept your word _____

_____

_____

_____ (66).

As per usual, _____

_____

_____ (196).

Jade

August 27, 2010

Mr. Burton Mannheim

Directorate of Operations, Central Intelligence Agency

Mr. Mannheim,

I am glad to hear that your youngest has successfully departed for college. When the time comes, I do have a suggestion for a fraternity with which I have an association. Just a thought. My best regards to Loretta.

Something has come up regarding one of my organization's projects. We are in search of _____

_____

_____

_____

_____

_____

_____ (9).

What I would like you to do is to _____

_____

_____

_____

_____

_____

_____ (234).

_____

_____

_____

_____ (90).

_____ (52).

_____ (11).

Ten seconds to the disappearance of this message.

Jade

September 12, 2010

Mr. Brandon Grave, 33rd Degree

Cryptographic Archivist

The Scottish Rite

Dear Mr. Grave,

I am sure that receiving an enciphered message like this will be something of a shock. _____

_____ (155).

_____

_____

_____

_____ (165). In addition, he had some books of yours on old Masonic ciphers. I thought you were the best person to receive a message enciphered with an antique Masonic cipher. I remember my grandfather speaking warmly of his Masonic and Scottish Rite associations. _____

_____

_____

_____

_____ (156).

_____

_____

_____

_____

_____ (23).

_____

_____

_____ (175).

_____

_____

_____

_____ (164).

_____

_____ (254).

_____

_____

_____

_____ (176). _____

_____

_____

_____

_____ (166).

I ask your help in this matter. _____

_____

_____ (203). If you would please
supply this person with a decrypted copy of this message

_____

_____

_____

_____ (153).

I know that this sounds crazy. Perhaps you can look up my
grandfather's name in some Scottish Rite directory, which will
verify that part of the story. _____

_____

_____ (216).

_____

_____ (99).

With hope,

Allison Carroll

_____

Mannheim:

There is little time.

_____

_____

_____ (77). _____

_____

_____

_____

_____(348).

_____

_____

_____(38).

_____

_____

_____

_____ (349).

_____

_____

_____

_____ (109).

_____ (350).

J.

September 23, 2010

Special Agent Georgette Grenfell

The Federal Bureau of Investigation

The United States Department of Justice

Ms. Grenfell,

_____

_____

_____

_____ (351)

The text of a plaque placed in a classified trophy room within the headquarters of the Central Intelligence Agency, Langley, Virginia.

_____

_____

_____

_____

_____

_____

_____

_____

_____ (39)

Chapter 4

Letter Substitution Cryptograms

Puzzle 1
Difficulty Level: Easy

B JFUJUCA NRYN SA HAAN

JAFCUEYDDZ NU YDDUS HA NU

PUEOAZ NU ZUW HZ JDYEC, HYJC,

YEM CU QUFNR.

Puzzle 2
Difficulty Level: Easy

DR UZKR XHGRRG RFPZJWXFURG

MVCQ NQRGRHPXZWF. EWRZFR PRWW

IR IVQR ZJVCP DUZP MVC DXFU PV

VBBRQ PV PUR FRQKXNR VB PUR

ZQIM VB UXF IZLRFPM PUR AXHO.

Puzzle 3

Difficulty Level: Easy

... SUUGTVYJF YKJ KJSF GI DJLXJY
TVYJMMTPJVLJ IGX YKJ HXTYTDK
WTMTYSXO IGXLJD ZKG SXJ ITPKYTVP
SPSTVDY YKJ LGMGVTSM USYXTGYD.

Puzzle 4

Difficulty Level: Easy

HJPJZNX NZPBXM SNE FJJP
EXKHSYJM OBZ LZBIBYKBP, NAADEJM
BO MKGJZYKPH IKXKYNZR ODPME OBZ
LJZEBPNX DEJ, NPM BYSJZQKEJ
KPEDXYJM FR SKE NEEBAKNYJE
NIBPH YSJ ZJFJX ABXBPKEYE

Puzzle 5

Difficulty Level: Easy

GUAW AWY KBLYEA TZ GKJ, AWY
KIYEBK TZ AWY NEUIWAC DQCA
FWKEIY. AWYUJ XQOSUF KFAULUAH
CWTQSB ZTFQC TE "XYKFY," TE
ZKEEUEI AWY ZSKDYC TZ CHDXKAWH
ZTJ AWY CTQAW KEB UAC FKQCY, TE
XJTDTAUEI AWY ITTB CYECY TZ
CSKLYJH.

Puzzle 6

Difficulty Level: Easy

CHA RNG LCIKLWKAZ DKIO C IKIVA
VKXA SNEAHTNH—NH DNGVZ
LNPAIOKTS VKXA "ZGXA" LGKI RNG
JAIIAH? DCLOKTSINT DNGVZ TNI
CUUAFI IOA IKIVA NW XKTS; K ZN TNI
OCEA OKL FHAQGZKUA CSCKTLI IKIVAL
NW TNJKVKIR—CTZ TAKIOAH, K IOKTX,
ZN RNG.

Puzzle 7

Difficulty Level: Easy

LXW Z DYYV TFPY HYYV, URHB X

HOZKLB DZB TFPY MZHZDOY, XTFVK

BLFHY QLF QYPY KXBLYPZVK XPTH

GFP TN SXRHY, BLYV BLXB SFRPB

QFROW LXMY SFVMZSBYW TY, XOO

BLFHY NYXPH XKF

Puzzle 8

Difficulty Level: Easy

T AZSD ZQFZEI CDDR TRMDVDIMDW

MH ADZV HG EHKV BTQTMZVE

DPJQHTMI, ZRW DIJDXTZQQE MH ADZV

HG EHKV BKXA QDII FDQQ-YRHFR

ZXMTSTMTDI TRSHQSTRO

YDRMKXYE-ZRW MAD YTRO HG IJZTR.

Puzzle 9

Difficulty Level: Easy

I LQVLDITDOIG LPD NW ILLPDL DJID

MIDPL VIFA DN DJP FOSOG YIH,

OTSNGSOTZ FIFJPL NW UHPFONQL

KPDIGL, UIHDOFQGIHGE ZNGM. YP

JISP I ZPTPHIG OMPI NW DJP

GNFIDONTL NW DJP KPDIGL

OTSNGSPM, ITM FIT UOT MNYT I FIFJP

DN YODJOT I DPT KOGP HIMOQL,

NWDPT GPLL-VQD DJID OL TND KQFJ

VPDDPH DJIT ATNYOTZ TNDJOTZ.

Puzzle 10

Difficulty Level: Easy

YMGPKMPBFI FIP SPQRTDP DBF

TYFZHGP WTYK BXBKFDPMF GTTK,

WTY SHQQ CHMG B DBMHQB

PMAPQTXP SHFI B CHQP

HMGHRBFHME SIPKP WTY RBM

GHZRTAPK PAHGPMRP TC DK.

IBQQHEBM'Z BRFHAHFHPZ.

Puzzle 11

Difficulty Level: Easy

EV EFCEBV, LYTHT CAFF WT E

VKWVLEOLAEF WTOTQAL LI BIK

NTHVIOEFFB EV CT HTMIJTH LYT

MEMYTV. NFTEVT RI LEUT SIHT LYEO

LYT KVKEF NHTMEKLAIOV LYEL BIKH

VLEQQ VKVNTMLV OILYAOD. LYIVT CYI

RI, A ES VIHHB LI VEB, SKVL WT

YEORFTR CALY TPLHTST NHTZKRAMT.

Puzzle 12

Difficulty Level: Easy

SPBU, SPBU UIPZX PLD, PX P

XITWZYAU VZITPWAYDB, XIEIZPG DC

AJI DVIZPAYEIX DC AJYX

DZLPBYNPAYDB PQDVAIQ TDGDZ

BPSIX PX TZUVADBUSX VIZJPVX DBI

QPU UDW XJPGG FI VPZA DC DWZ

DZLPBYNPAYDB, PBQ JPEI XWTJ P

TZUVADBUS UDWZXIGC.

Puzzle 13

Difficulty Level: Easy

AO HXW NXWCE NAQ S JSQ MX HXWI
USWYP, OAIYM UXQGAQUP FAJ MFSM
HXW SIP FAY YAQUPIP OIAPQE.
MFPIPAQ AY S EIXB XO FXQPH MFSM
USMUFPY FAY FPSIM, NFAUF, YSH
NFSM FP NACC, AY MFP TIPSM
FATFIXSE MX FAY IPSYXQ, SQE NFAUF,
XQUP TSAQPE, HXW NACC OAQE RWM
CAMMCP MIXWRCP AQ UXQGAQUAQT
FAJ XO MFP VWYMAUP XO HXWI
USWYP, AO AQEPPE MFSM USWYP AY
IPSCCH S TXXE XQP. SRISFSJ
CAQUXCQ

Puzzle 14

Difficulty Level: Easy

EKREISPJIRN AVBNBRD JSG NSZI S
UKMN KQ QKVJM. FIVUSFM BNM
KPHIMN ZRKAR SFFPBESNBKR BM
QKYRH BR NUI SREBIRN HIWBEI KQ
AVBNBRD S MIEVIN JIMMSDI KR NUI
UISH KQ S MPSWI SRH HBMFSNEUBRD
NUI MPSWI ABNU UBM
EKJJYRBESNBKR SQNIV UBM
DVKABRD USBV USH EKWIVIH NUI
AVBNBRD. UIPIR QKYEUI DSBRIM

Puzzle 15

Difficulty Level: Easy

JARVYVP LVPSVBJ SLDSVLJU. JAVU
IVLVNU ORPA JAV SLDSVLJU JD
XVBDIV JAVRL SLDSVLJU JAEJ JAVU
IEU IDLV SVLHVBJNU LVPSVBJ RJ. K W
BAVPJVLJDG

Puzzle 16

Difficulty Level: Easy

K RID FKD ID IBOLTJDG MD IDA
GMZKR, IOIKDNG IDA MZZMDJDG.
ZJMZVJ YDMF GXKN, IDQ NGJJB RVJIB
ME TJ IG ZIBGKJN. MEGJD, IN I NKOD
ME GXJKB OBJIG BJNZJRG, GXJA
QMD'G JUJD KDUKGJ TJ. QIUJ WIBBA

Puzzle 17

Difficulty Level: Tricky

G FQXM QHWIFMV CQT GHIW
RKGHIWH'D IMHI, CFGRF G FQXM
LMMH JMXMKWBGHS AWV DWNM
IGNM.

Puzzle 18

Difficulty Level: Tricky

PU ENGMQ YK YKBU UN ZLNJKKQ
EPUDNGU QKMRW EPUD FW ZMRS UN
UGLS UDPB BULNSXDNMQ NTKL UN
DPB FRCKBUW.

Puzzle 19

Difficulty Level: Tricky

... ANQZYKI LSVL LSB DKYLBK NZ LSVL

IBGGVCB YG YQFBBF LSB BGLBBIBF

CBQBKVX VKQNXF, MYALNK NZ LSB

HVLLXB NZ GVKVLNCV.

Puzzle 20

Difficulty Level: Tricky

NY. VSJYVS U. O. MKTIOSX PJ ZSYBS

WZ PCS OSWNSY WEN EJGKEWO

LJAENSY JL PCWP VYJAR

Puzzle 21

Difficulty Level: Tricky

This cipher has a keyword that's also the blank word in the message.

IPXZPT ESXQACG'B "SLDMBSPL" PO

_ _ _ _ _ _ UMB WLTCASCDCIAG

ISBMBZTPWB. TCHAMXC NSR MB NCMI

PO ZNC QLSKNZB PO ZNC KPAICL

XSTXAC.

Puzzle 22

Difficulty Level: Tricky

This cipher has a keyword that's also the blank word in the message.

QTIY XKAPIOW, TYG TE WM

OUUTJYGML, LITVFN RG PYTXY UT

MTV OL "_ _ _ _ _ _"; LITVFN K YTU RG

ORFG UT GLAOCG WM AVJJGYU

CJGNKAOWGYU, MTV LIOFF JGCTJU

UT IKW.

Puzzle 23

Difficulty Level: Tricky

This cipher has a keyword that's also the blank word in the message.

J BF BL OFVHIMOO JL SYO

TJEORSIEBSO IN IVOEBSJILW JL SYO

ROLSEBH JLSOHHJAOLRO BAOLRM.

FM WXVOEQJWIE JW ILO _ _ _ _ _ _

FBLLYOJF. FM INNJRO YBLTHOW SYO

IVOEBSJILW IN NJOHT IVOEBSJQOW -

UBWJRBHHM, WVJOW - JL ROESBJL

HIRBSJILW BEIXLT SYO PIEHT.

Puzzle 24

Difficulty Level: Tricky

KHD XSQI ZOIFRZLZIO THQZIR SFO

HRXIM YHVVDFZTR SWIFRT SR RXI

OIGSMRVIFRT HL TRSRI, OILIFTI,

ZFRIMZHM, SFO RMSFTGHMRSRZHF

Puzzle 25

Difficulty Level: Tricky

J CIPT JI QZOGJWFYZO GBZG APF

BZHV Z DGOPIX LVDJOV GP DVOHV

APFO WPFIGOA, GP QOPGVWG APFO

WPFIGOA NOPR VIVRA ZXVIGD, JI

QZOGJWFYZO GP QOPGVWG APFO

WPFIGOA NOPR LPFUYV ZXVIGD,

Puzzle 26

Difficulty Level: Tricky

JCS PMKHJ UDBMZRJMUF UP JCS

GSVUFHJKRJUK MH JU DS BSZMDBS.

VMHH VRFFSKH IRFFUJ HXVLRJCMYS

QMJC R IRWHS QCUHS HMZFH HCS

IRFFUJ VRTS UWJ SOSF QMJC CSK

ZBRHHSH UF. NWGMJC VRKJMF

Puzzle 27

Difficulty Level: Tricky

KUV NTZBH PX HPIPHVH PDKT FVTFBV

NUT HT KUPDWX EDH FVTFBV NUT

WVK KUV OZVHPK. KZR, PY RTJ OED,

KT GVBTDW KT KUV YPZXK OBEXX.

KUVZV'X YEZ BVXX OTSFVKPKPTD.

HNPWUK STZZTN

Puzzle 28

Difficulty Level: Tricky

OLHUFWL USLBH DZIP HLJLZBS ID RFH

BFOLH, FEGSMOFEY RBPFSWIE WRBW

BEOZL NL LALGMWLO NX DFZFEY

HVMBO BH NLDFWH B HISOFLZ,

CBHRFEYWIE IZOLZLO WRBW RL NL

RBEYLO BH B HUX. RL CBH EIW FE B

HLEWFPLEWBS IZ YLELZIMH PIIO.

(TIHLUR T. LSSFH, RFH LAGLSSLEGX:

YLIZYL CBHRFEYWIE, 2008, U. 129)

Puzzle 29

Difficulty Level: Treacherous

This cipher has a keyword. See whether you can discover it!

IPRPQWD KWGNFRIHJR, KP NWZP FR

JBQ SBGHJTA XWCJQ CJNR WRTQP,

JBH JO BRFOJQX, KNJ KWG

FRHPQSPYHPT RPWQ HWQQAHJKR

HJTWA JR HNP KWA HJ EQFHFGN

DFRPG.

Puzzle 30

Difficulty Level: Treacherous

We removed all the spaces and punctuation in this cipher.
Use letter frequency analysis to crack the code.

YBEUU QDJYI GEDSG MQDAD JQPIF

QFYDJ EOSQE PSQHY KFGDS IEDBE

UUYDJ QPGDB FGQOI FQBED IGDQD

IYXYP UVXQI YXXUQ DTDEH ZVIFQ

KQRPQ KQDIK IFYIU PKYX GBQBY

PPEXX JGJPG KTFQP XGOQO EPIFQ

BYAKQ EOOPQ QJEUG DIFQK QPMGB

QEOFQ PBEAD IPVIF QADGI QJKIY

IQKEO YUQPG BYHFG BFGKQ IQPDY

XXVSP YIQOA XIFEA SFIFQ KQIFY

DTKUA KIZQT QRIKQ BPQIE APSPY

IGIAJ QKFYX XXYKI YKXED SYKEA

POPQQ JEU

Puzzle 31

Difficulty Level: Treacherous

Z NEX QPB OP WZAT ENJT CNEENWT

OP LQ KZJT CTWWQ NSI LQ MYZRIUTS,

OP CTWWQ'E JNLZRQ ZS

CYZRNITRCYZN.

Puzzle 32

Difficulty Level: Treacherous
This puzzle has a keyword. See whether you can discover it!

VHZQ GOXHQ OWEQA - DOZUBY, JKPA

BOJA, KW DKMKJKOW DJHYBAI

RABKWE AWAGV JKWAI - YBA GOQP HL

O ITV - IBOJJ GAAY YBA IOGA LOYA, RV

YBA QZJAI HL SOQ.

Puzzle 33

Difficulty Level: Treacherous

We removed all the spaces and punctuation in this cipher.
Use letter frequency analysis to crack the code.

EQQSL LKJMB SOTTQE VOKQS LMETO

TQSLK MYEJB MCJTS OTQLK QEKJY

MULTE XEVQS LREGE UEKJO TEZZL

EGTBG MYTON SQFAQ RMKQO KALTO

QTWMA GKLVO KTOCL KRL

Puzzle 34

Difficulty Level: Treacherous

TIUUILHKE SVXRH

OLIHRSIEB

BCI PKEUISILVBI HBVBIH KU VDILRPV

Puzzle 35

Difficulty Level: Treacherous

This cipher has a keyword that's also the blank word in the message.

S CTPR YCR ABRQQSLF DN T NDGWRG

VDWWTLESLF DNNSVRG DN KDJGQ YD

VDWWJLSVTYR YD KDJ T GRMJRQY

NDG TQQSQYTLVR. SN KDJ VTL QHTGR

TL CDJG DG YZD NDG VDLPRGQTYSDL

DL T WTYYRG DN WJYJTB SLYRGRQY,

S TQO KDJG SLEJBFRLVR YD WRRY

WR YDWDGGDZ LSFCY TY CRGDL'Q

_ _ _ _ _ _ , LDY NTG NGDW KDJG

BDEFSLFQ, ARFSLLSLF TY RSFCY H.W.

Puzzle 36

Difficulty Level: Treacherous

This cipher has a keyword that's also the blank word in the message.

BTZCNDBTHDMVA, J LHTTCD JFKMEM

ACB, MJDYMN. J YHWM TC KNCCZ CZ

CBN LCTWMNXHDJCT. DYJX TCDM

SJVV OM VMZD JT H OCDDVM JT H

_ _ _ _ JT H DNMM; J YHWM TC SHA DC

EJNMLD DYM HBDYCNJDJMX DC ACB.

XC, HVV J LHT EC JX NMZBXM ACB,

HTE DYHD J EC JNNMWCLHOVA.

Puzzle 37

Difficulty Level: Treacherous

TN TJ EAFETSZ NVSN YK APZG TL

NVTJ TRGLNTQTESNTPL LPN MG

YGLNTPLGR NP KPFA EPZZGSIFGJ PA

JFWGATPAJ. T SY TL SL GONAGYGZK

JGLJTNTHG WPJTNTPL NVSN YFJN LPN

MG EPYWAPYTJGR.

Puzzle 38

Difficulty Level: Treacherous

EWKYK OTD ANKTYNZ EGG LPAW GS T

EYTFN NKSE RZ EWK DTEKNNFEK

YKBGDFEFGQFQH EG WTMK SPNNZ

AGMKYKC ZGPY EYTAXD.

Puzzle 39
Difficulty Level: Treacherous

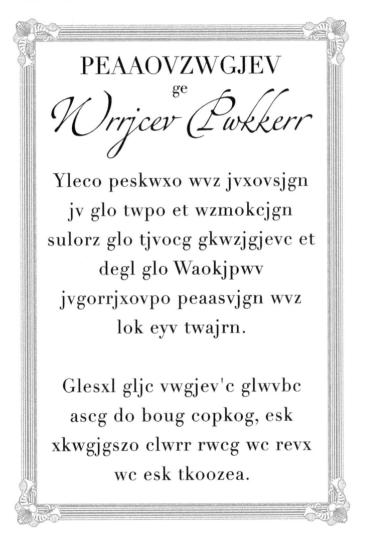

PEAAOVZWGJEV

ge

Wrrjcev Pwkkerr

Yleco peskwxo wvz jvxovsjgn
jv glo twpo et wzmokcjgn
sulorz glo tjvocg gkwzjgjevc et
degl glo Waokjpwv
jvgorrjxovpo peaasvjgn wvz
lok eyv twajrn.

Glesxl gljc vwgjev'c glwvbc
ascg do boug copkog, esk
xkwgjgszo clwrr rwcg wc revx
wc esk tkoozea.

Puzzle 40

Difficulty Level: Treacherous

B EFZFWBSH KAMSBWFKV FVQKZQML
JMGMAWFKV. MQMV WPKYOP HKY BSM
GKEAMWMVW, BAAMBS WK NM
FVGKEAMWMVW. WPKYOP
MDDMGWFQM, BAAMBS WK NM
FVMDDMGWFQM. LYV WXY (~400 NG)

Puzzle 41

Difficulty Level: Treacherous
This puzzle has a keyword. See whether you can discover it!

Y EQTJCS XJ Y WYT FVC UTCFJ WCSQ
OVYT VQ OVXTUJ LCG CGMVO OC.
PYGSQTEQ N DQOQS

Puzzle 42

Difficulty Level: Treacherous

VP VW K JKVG WMZZKGA RJ OVWPRGA

PR WKA POKP POI WKJIQMKGBW RJ

EVSIGPA OKLI SIID JRGQIB VD

XRDPGRLIGWVIW VDLRELVDQ DRP

LIGA DVXI NIRNEI. JIEVY

JGKDHJMGPIG

Chapter 5

Number Substitution Cryptograms

Puzzle 43
Difficulty Level: Easy

... 23.26.13.25.17.06.17.22.01 16.11.10

05.26.17.16.17.12.11 03.17.16.11

09.17.02.17.16.07.26.24

17.22.14.13.26.09.07.16.17.13.22

07.05.13.18.16 16.11.10

07.09.10.26.17.08.07.22

23.07.16.26.17.13.16.12'

08.13.22.16.17.22.10.22.16.07.02

07.26.09.24, 12.18.08.11 07.12

16.11.10 12.17.19.10 07.22.06

02.13.08.07.16.17.13.22 13.14

01.26.13.18.23.12 13.14

08.13.22.16.17.22.10.22.16.07.02

07.26.09.24 16.26.13.13.23.12.

Puzzle 44

Difficulty Level: Easy

XX.VIII.V XXIII.XV.XVIII.IV XX.VIII.I.XX

XXIII.V VIII.I.XXII.V VI.XVIII.XV.XIII

XIII.XXI.XII.XX.IX.XVI.XII.V

I.VII.V.XIV.XX.XIX XVI.XII.I.III.V.IV

IX.XIV XX.VIII.V III.I.XIII.XVI XV.VI

XX.VIII.V II.XVIII.IX.XX.IX.XIX.VIII,

XXIII.XV.XVIII.XI.IX.XIV.VII

IX.XIV.IV.V.XVI.V.XIV.IV.V.XIV.XX.XII.XXV

XV.VI XV.XIV.V I.XIV.XV.XX.VIII.V.XVIII,

I.XII.XII XVI.XV.IX.XIV.XX.XIX XX.XV

XX.VIII.V XIX.I.XIII.V

III.XV.XIV.III.XII.XXI.XIX.IX.XV.XIV.

Puzzle 45
Difficulty Level: Easy

20.18.04.26.22.04 22.04.01.17 02.22

01.16.19.14.11.04 26.22 19.16

09.12.04.19.12.04.10 19.12.14.22

16.24.24.04.10 14.22

26.11.11.04.20.19.26.25.18.04 19.16

23.16.02, 26.18.16.01.21 09.14.19.12

23.16.02.10 20.18.26.01.22 19.16

19.02.10.01 16.06.04.10 09.04.22.19

20.16.14.01.19.

Puzzle 46
Difficulty Level: Easy

15.24.14.18 14.18 16

23.05.19.18.21.05.04

25.13.16.03.09.21.09 18.21.23.03.21.15

12.14.15.24.14.17 15.24.21

14.17.17.21.03 23.14.03.23.05.21 19.11

25.21.17.21.03.16.05 18.14.03

24.21.17.03.04 23.05.14.17.15.19.17, 16

25.03.19.13.06 15.24.16.15 26.04

16.25.21.17.15.18 23.16.17.17.19.15

06.21.17.21.15.03.16.15.21.

Puzzle 47

Difficulty Level: Easy

08.01, 05.04.09, 20 25.18.08.06 08.07 13.01.04

10.17.26.18.09 13.01.26.13 05.08.11 01.26.23 13.08

23.04.17.20.19.04.22 25.04.18.13.11.24.25.05 13.08

09.10.26.20.18. 20 25.18.08.06 26 15.22.04.26.13

02.26.18.05 13.01.20.18.15.09 13.01.26.13 26.22.04

18.08.13 06.20.23.04.17.05 25.18.08.06.18,

20.18.24.17.11.23.20.18.15 05.08.11.22

09.04.24.22.04.13

22.04.18.11.18.24.20.26.13.20.08.18 08.07

26.02.04.22.20.24.26.18

24.20.13.20.12.04.18.09.01.20.10, 13.01.04

08.26.13.01 08.07 26.17.17.04.15.20.26.18.24.04

13.01.26.13 05.08.11 02.26.23.04 13.08 13.01.04

09.10.26.18.20.09.01 13.01.22.08.18.04, 26.18.23

13.01.04 26.18.18.11.26.17 10.04.18.09.20.08.18

13.01.26.13 05.08.11 22.04.24.04.20.19.04

07.22.08.02 02.26.23.22.20.23.

Puzzle 48

Difficulty Level: Easy

05.19.11.24 11.24.09

12.03.15.13.19.12.11.19.03.15 03.26

13.10.22.22.10.15.18.19.16.24.10.04

11.24.19.25 05.09.09.01 26.03.06

"20.11.11.09.06.19.15.16

18.19.25.22.03.17.10.22

25.09.15.11.19.04.09.15.11.25", 05.09

15.09.09.18 11.03 12.24.10.15.16.09

11.10.12.11.19.12.25 10.15.18

25.11.06.10.11.09.16.19.08.09 26.03.06

11.24.09 22.10.06.16.09.06

07.19.12.11.20.06.09.

Puzzle 49

Difficulty Level: Easy

49 42.02 67.49.36.60.15.91.33.57.33.67,

42.50.67 62.63.42.62

73.49.88.83.49.50.36.15.50 49.36

36.33.62 62.15 62.33.36.62.49.35.64

42.46.42.49.50.36.62 02.33. 50.15.50.33

15.35 62.63.33 57.33.36.62 15.35

64.15.96 42.57.33 83.50.15.73.50,

42.50.67 36.15 49.62 36.63.42.88.88

57.33.02.42.49.50.

Puzzle 50

Difficulty Level: Easy

21.02.22.04.05.24.18 06.14.12.13

13.01.02.07.04 13.01.20.13 13.01.24

24.12.13.20.21.05.02.12.01.06.24.07.13

08.25 13.01.24 04.07.02.26.01.13.12

08.25 13.01.24 26.08.05.23.24.07

22.02.11.22.05.24 02.12 01.02.12

08.16.07 21.11.20.02.07.22.01.02.05.23.

Puzzle 51

Difficulty Level: Easy

13.18. 08.01.12.12.09.07.01.14 08.01.19

02.05.05.14 19.05.18.22.09.14.07 01.19

01 04.15.21.02.12.05 01.07.05.14.20

06.15.18 20.08.05 19.15.22.09.05.20

21.14.09.15.14 06.15.18 13.01.14.25

25.05.01.18.19, 09.14 23.08.09.03.08

16.15.19.09.20.09.15.14 08.05 08.01.19

03.15.13.16.18.15.13.09.19.05.04

13.01.14.25 04.05.12.09.03.01.20.05

04.09.16.12.15.13.01.20.09.03

14.05.07.15.20.09.01.20.09.15.14.19.

Puzzle 52

Difficulty Level: Easy

15 12.07.09.08 21.25.06.21

02.19.21.06.17.12.15.07.20

15.07.21.19.14.14.15.20.19.07.24.19

17.06.21.19.14.14.15.21.19.17 09.18.19.02

06.10.19.02.15.24.06.07 17.09.15.14 15.17 06

17.19.07.17.15.21.15.18.19 15.17.17.16.19. 15

17.16.20.20.19.17.21 21.25.06.21 11.09.16

02.19.21.06.17.12 21.25.19

17.06.21.19.14.14.15.21.19.17 15.07

17.16.24.25 06 08.06.11 21.25.06.21

21.25.19.11 25.06.18.19 21.09 26.14.11

09.18.19.02 06.10.19.02.15.24.06.07

21.19.02.02.15.21.09.02.11 21.09 09.21.25.19.02

14.09.24.06.21.15.09.07.17; 21.25.19

17.24.06.07.17 24.06.07 21.25.19.07 01.19

23.19.02.26.09.02.10.19.05 15.07

23.06.17.17.15.07.20, 06.17 15.21 08.19.02.19.

Puzzle 53

Difficulty Level: Easy

... 97.39.34.13 37.91.41.06.08.71.34.65.34.37

97.39.34 56.34.77 34.71.91.37.34.56.06.34

97.39.92.97 91 78.83.92.56.97.34.37 91.56

39.92.83.83.91.87.92.56'41 39.08.53.34 92.56.37

08.80.80.91.06.34, 92.41 97.39.34.13 39.92.37

37.91.41.06.08.71.34.65.34.37 77.39.92.97 91

78.83.92.56.97.34.37 34.92.65.83.91.34.65 91.56

97.39.34 53.08.56.97.39.

Puzzle 54

Difficulty Level: Easy

XXVI-III-VIII VI-XX-XXII-XXII IV-XI-X
XVII-XXV-VI-VII-VIII-XIX X-XVII
XXVI-III-XXV-XIII
XX-XXI-XXVI-VIII-XII-XVIII-XI-XI-XVIII,
II-III-VIII-XVIII XIII-XI-IX-VIII-XI-XVIII-VIII
XX-XIII-VII-VIII-XIX XXI-XI-XII XX
XVIII-XI-XVIII-VIII-XV-XXV-XIII-XXVI-VIII-
XVIII-XXVI XI-XXI-XXI-XXV-VI-VIII,
II-XX-XIII XVII-XXII-XX-VI-VIII-XIX XIV-IV
XI-XVIII-VIII XI-XXI IX-IV
XX-XIII-XIII-XI-VI-XXV-XX-XXVI-VIII-XIII;
XXVI-III-VIII XII-VIII-VI-XI-XII-XIX XI-XXI
XXVI-III-XX-XXVI VI-XX-XXII-XXII
II-XXV-XXII-XXII
XIII-X-XIV-XIII-XXVI-XX-XVIII-XXVI-XXV-
XX-XXVI-VIII IV-XI-X-XII
XIII-XXVI-XI-XII-IV XX-XIV-XI-X-XXVI
XX-XVIII XX-XVIII-XI-XVIII-IV-IX-XI-X-XIII
XXVI-VIII-XXII-VIII-XVII-III-XI-XVIII-VIII
XXVI-XXV-XVII.

Puzzle 55

Difficulty Level: Easy

26.11 11.18.02.22.10 16.06.12.09

22.05.22.04.16 18.05.21 16.06.12.09

23.09.26.22.05.21, 14.06.09.02.26.05.24

11.06.24.22.11.25.22.09, 11.06

25.12.09.11 16.06.12 11.06 11.25.22

25.22.18.09.11: 11.25.22 06.05.22 11.06

10.03.18.05.21.22.09 16.06.12 18.05.21

11.25.22 06.11.25.22.09 11.06 24.22.11

11.25.22 05.22.14.10 11.06 16.06.12.

04.18.09.02 11.14.18.26.05

Puzzle 56

Difficulty Level: Easy

IX-VI I XIX-V-III-XVIII-V-XX

XVI-IX-V-III-V XV-VI XIV-V-XXIII-XIX

IX-XIX IV-IX-XXII-XXI-XII-VII-V-IV

II-XXV I XIX-XVI-XXV

II-V-VI-XV-XVIII-V XX-VIII-V

XX-IX-XIII-V IX-XIX XVIII-IX-XVI-V ,

VIII-V XIII-XXI-XIX-XX II-V XVI-XXI-XX

XX-XV IV-V-I-XX-VIII

XX-XV-VII-V-XX-VIII-V-XVIII

XXIII-IX-XX-VIII XX-VIII-V XIII-I-XIV

XX-XV XXIII-VIII-XV-XIII XX-VIII-V

XIX-V-III-XVIII-V-XX XXIII-I-XIX

XX-XV-XII-IV . XIX-XXI-XIV XX-XXVI-XXI

Puzzle 57

Difficulty Level: Easy

98.41.66.98.70.28.70.61.37.70 :

12.14.70.12 53.41.70.61.13.14 66.73

12.14.27 70.41.12 66.73 65.93.68.61.28

18.14.68.13.14 13.66.61.47.68.47.12.47

68.61 46.27.41.93 61.27.70.41.65.93

37.27.13.27.68.46.68.61.28 93.66.35.41

73.41.68.27.61.37.47 18.68.12.14.66.35.12

56.35.68.12.27 37.27.13.27.68.46.68.61.28

93.66.35.41 27.61.27.67.68.27.47.

73.41.70.61.13.68.47 67

13.66.41.61.73.66.41.37

Puzzle 58

Difficulty Level: Easy

19.73.22 26.27.48.02.32.64 41.28.18

19.73.22.18 28.23.22

03.22.19.19.32.91.03

64.18.91.32.64.28.02 28.48.42.27.19

26.42.02.32.19.32.64.32.28.91.41;

19.73.22.18 41.73.42.27.02.87

73.22.28.23 73.42.35

26.42.02.32.19.32.64.32.28.91.41

19.28.02.65 28.48.42.27.19 19.73.22.86.

03.22.42.23.03.22 35.22.02.87.42.91

Puzzle 59

Difficulty Level: Tricky

... 88.77.08.88.67.77.30.82

02.53.53.08.16.85.32.36.85.91 56.08.77

04.36.70 67.24.88.67.85.70.67.70

33.04.36.30.67 56.36.91.04.32.36.85.91

36.85 53.02.85.02.25.02, 67.80.67.85

32.04.08.16.91.04 02.77.85.08.30.25'70

77.67.53.67.36.88.32.70 33.67.77.67

30.08.70.32 36.85 27.02.32.32.30.67

Puzzle 60

Difficulty Level: Tricky

...19.25.13.19.10.21.02.14.16.03.19.15.02

16.13.15 02.10.19.23 16.02 14.22

19.22.21.11.15.17 21.15 14.22

13.15.19.22.03.02.25.07.15.13 21.05

11.22.02.25.14.25.22.03. 25 03.22.09

09.25.02.23 14.22 06.13.22.16.19.23

14.23.15 11.22.02.02.25.06.25.17.25.14.05

22.18 19.23.16.03.12.25.03.12 21.05

16.17.17.15.12.25.16.03.19.15 14.22

14.23.15 02.25.07.15 22.18 23.25.02

21.16.08.15.02.14.05 14.23.15

04.25.03.12.

Puzzle 61

Difficulty Level: Tricky

61.76.98 52.21.63.63

21.97.97.79.04.21.51.68.79.63.61

58.79.22.04 70.51.68.43.76.63.58 68.76

58.79.51.43.67.59 52.21.68.59.76.98.68

43.51.21.58.21.22.91 51.63.51.43.97

68.59.79 51.43.79.51 11.43.76.97

52.79.58.68 70.76.21.22.68,

58.76.98.68.59 70.51.58.68

68.51.43.43.61.68.76.52.22, 11.43.76.97

58.79.70.68.79.97.16.79.43

68.52.79.22.68.61-11.21.43.58.68

68.59.43.76.98.91.59 68.59.79

68.52.79.22.68.61-22.21.22.68.59.

Puzzle 62

Difficulty Level: Tricky

02.12.06, 26.13.23 07.19.22 09.22.08.07

12.21 07.19.22 08.11.22.24.07.09.06.14

26.20.22.13.07.08−09.22.23,

02.22.15.15.12.04, 25.15.06.22,

12.09.26.13.20.22, 26.13.23 26.15.15

07.19.22 09.22.08.07−26.08 04.22.15.15

26.08 14.02.08.22.15.21 26.09.22

07.19.22 18.13.13.22.09

24.18.09.24.15.22.

Puzzle 63

Difficulty Level: Tricky

27.60.01.14 01 47.32.01.50.01.14.73.74

47.84.01.14.60! 01.64 01.48

01.14.14.41.32.48.84.99 80.41.32 14.60.84

47.84.80.84.48.64.84 73.48 01 50.89.32.47.84.32

74.01.64.84, 74.67.84.50.84.48.14 14.32.73.84.64

14.41 32.84-84.48.01.74.14 14.60.84

64.60.41.41.14.73.48.09 73.48 01.48

01.14.14.84.50.05.14 14.41 64.60.41.27 60.41.27

14.60.84 90.73.74.14.73.50 60.01.47

01.74.14.89.01.67.67.99 64.60.41.14

60.73.50.64.84.67.80 45.99

01.74.74.73.47.84.48.14-01.48.47

74.67.84.50.84.48.14 05.32.41.74.84.84.47.64

14.41 64.60.41.41.14 60.73.50.64.84.67.80 45.99

01.74.74.73.47.84.48.14!

Puzzle 64

Difficulty Level: Tricky

94.92.73 10.45.99 78.76 53.92.63.10 69

85.73.99.27 94.92.69.85

10.73.85.85.45.34.73 85.92.45.67.67

78.73 76.63.75.54 67.69.45.69.85.63.99

53.69.94.92 10.73.

Puzzle 65

Difficulty Level: Tricky

III-VIII-XVIII-XXIV-XVII III VIII-XXIV-XIX

XXIII-XXIV-III-XVII-XVI XXI-VIII VIII-X-XXIV-XXII-II

XXIV-XV-VII-XXIV-XVII-X-XXIV-IV-XIV-XXIV,

XIX-X-XVIII-XI XXIII-XXI-I-XVII VIII-XII-X

XVII-XXIV-XIV-XXI-XVII-II XXI-VIII

XIV-III-XVIII-XIV-XI-X-IV-XXVI II-XXI-I-XII-XXII-XXIV

III-XXVI-XXIV-IV-XVIII-XVI, XXIII-XXI-I XIX-XXI-I-XXII-II

XII-XXIV III IV-III-XVIII-I-XVII-III-XXII VIII-XXI-XVII III

XVIII-XVII-III-IV-XVI-VIII-XXIV-XVII XVIII-XXI XVIII-XI-XXIV

XXI-VIII-VIII-X-XIV-XXIV XXI-VIII XVIII-XI-XXIV

II-X-XVII-XXIV-XIV-XVIII-XXI-XVII-III-XVIII-XXIV XXI-VIII

X-IV-XVIII-XXIV-XXII-XXII-X-XXVI-XXIV-IV-XIV-XXIV

XVIII-XI-III-XVIII VIII-XXI-XIV-I-XVI-XXIV-XVI XXI-IV

XIV-XXI-I-IV-XVIII-XXIV-XVII-X-IV-XVIII-XXIV-XXII-XXII-X-

XXVI-XXIV-IV-XIV-XXIV.

Puzzle 66

Difficulty Level: Tricky

... 21.11.15 15.11 24.13.17.21.15 11.03.03

15.06.23 05.11.18.24.25.15.23.13

20.05.13.23.23.21 11.21 14.06.17.05.06

18.26 18.23.20.20.02.12.23.20

02.24.24.23.02.13. 26.11.25.13

05.02.13.23.03.25.22

02.15.15.23.21.15.17.11.21 15.11

03.11.22.22.11.14

01.23.15.02.17.22.23.01

17.21.20.15.13.25.05.15.17.11.21.20

02.20 01.17.05.15.02.15.23.01 15.11

26.11.25 18.02.09.23.20 26.11.25 02

04.23.13.26 04.02.22.25.02.10.22.23

02.20.20.23.15 17.21 02.21.26

11.13.12.02.21.17.08.02.15.17.11.21.

Puzzle 67

Difficulty Level: Tricky

00.50.57 17.49.58.99.00

37.49.45.57.58.80.33.57.80.00 81.99

49.22.00.57.80 00.50.57 33.49.99.00

33.49.58.28.39. 49.80.57

62.49.33.95.49.99.57.91 49.22

62.11.80.81.62.99 81.99 49.22.00.57.80

45.57.58.11 00.49.39.57.58.28.80.00

28.80.91 50.66.33.28.80.57. 09.66.00

17.50.57.80 22.28.80.28.00.81.62.99

28.58.57 49.80 00.49.95

00.50.57.58.57 81.99 80.49

39.81.33.81.00 00.49

49.95.95.58.57.99.99.81.49.80.

50 39 33.57.80.62.86.57.80

Puzzle 68

Difficulty Level: Tricky

12.15.83.34.45.68.25

34.29.14.03.12.29.83 21.83 34.12.14.34

53.29.01 14.01.52 01.14.34.15.45.01.83

50.29.12.14.35.29 49.15.83.29.51.25

45.01.03.29 34.12.29.25 12.14.35.29

29.37.12.14.21.83.34.29.52 14.51.51

45.34.12.29.68

14.51.34.29.68.01.14.34.15.35.29.83.

14.50.50.14 29.50.14.01

Puzzle 69

Difficulty Level: Tricky

02.23.18.17.18 09.17.18 09

02.18.17.17.21.16.22.18 22.05.02 05.13

22.21.18.03 14.05.21.24.14

09.17.05.19.24.11 02.23.18

26.05.17.22.11, 09.24.11 02.23.18

26.05.17.03.02 05.13 21.02 21.03

23.09.22.13 05.13 02.23.18.25

09.17.18 02.17.19.18.

26.21.24.03.02.05.24

12.23.19.17.12.23.21.22.22

Puzzle 70

Difficulty Level: Treacherous

34 97.65.45.20.15.67.90 65.96.67

56.34.01.01 50.67.81.81.28

01.40.34.50.50.67.96 32.40.34.51.67 34

32.99.01 01.15.99.15.34.65.96.67.90

34.96 50.40.34.51.99.90.67.51.50.40.34.99.

15.40.34.01 32.65.45.51.90 09.67

15.40.67 01.99.56.67 50.67.81.81.28

01.40.34.50.50.67.96 32.40.65 34.01

28.65.45.20 32.34.33.67.

Puzzle 71

Difficulty Level: Treacherous

VI-XVI VI VIII-XXII-XXVI-IX-XII-XXII-XVII-VI-XXVI

XVII-XX-XVI-XXII-XII-XIX, XXI-XIX

X-XXI-IV-XV-XVI-XXII XXV VIII-XXV-XIII-XXII

XVI-VI-XIX-XXII II-VI-XVI-XVI-VI-VIII-XXII IX-XXI

XX-XXI-IV-XV VII-XXV-XIX-XXII VI-XXVI-XIV

XIX-VI-XVII-XXV-XII-XX.

Puzzle 72

Difficulty Level: Treacherous

77.32.88 46.91.97.99 26.32

31.99.16.88.59.91.59.45.32.26 59.32

48.99.89.99.26.48. 77.32.88.31

89.91.61.45.90.77 50.45.90.90

25.88.89.89.99.31 59.46.99

45.86.26.32.61.45.26.77 77.32.88

46.91.97.99 04.31.32.88.86.46.59

88.16.32.26 77.32.88.31 26.91.61.99,

89.32.31 26.32.50, 91.26.48 89.32.31

91.90.50.91.77.25.

Puzzle 73

Difficulty Level: Treacherous

All the spaces and punctuation have been removed. Use letter frequency analysis to crack the code.

73 42 57 37 59 42 57 10 34 37 59 42 11

32 01 34 11 97 57 24 97 29 37 97 10 32

10 56 37 59 42 57 29 10 37 37 97 57 59

11 97 37 42 59 04 57 56 04 29 97 25 97

37 97 42 57 59 42 11 42 04 32 24 37 59

42 11 42 37 59 11 10 34 92 59 10 34 37

13 04 32 73 57 37 04 37 42 57 04 32 24

37 42 11 11 97 37 10 11 97 42 57 10 56

37 59 42 29 10 34 32 37 11 73

Puzzle 74

Difficulty Level: Treacherous

XI-XIII-VIII-XXI-XIII-III-XXIV-II-X-XI,

XI-XXV-XVIII-XIII X-XI-XIII

XVII-XXVI-V-XIX-I-XXI

XXIV-II-VI-XXV-VIII-I-XX-XXV-X-I-XXIV-VIII

XXII-VIII-XXIV-XV-VIII XXV-XIV X-XI-XIII

"XXIV-II-VII-XIII-II XXIV-III X-XI-XIII

XIV-XXIV-VIII-XIV XXIV-III

XIX-I-V-XIII-II-X-XXIII".

Puzzle 75

Difficulty Level: Treacherous

XXIII-V XVII-V-II-VIII-VI XXIV-V-II XIII-III-XX-XX

XI-III-XXIII-XVII III-VI

I-II-XXVI-XV-XXVI-III-I-III-XXIII-XXI VI-V I-XII-XII

XXII-XII XIV-V-XXII-XXII-II-XXIII-III-XIV-XVI-VI-XII

XIII-III-VI-IX XXIV-V-II III-XXIII

XIV-III-XV-IX-XII-XXVI. III XVI-I-I-II-XXVI-XII

XXIV-V-II VI-IX-XVI-VI XXII-XXIV

III-XXIII-VI-XII-XXIII-VI-III-V-XXIII-I XVI-XXVI-XII

XXII-V-I-VI IX-V-XXIII-V-XXVI-XVI-VIII-XX-XII.

Puzzle 76

Difficulty Level: Treacherous

All the spaces and punctuation have been removed, and the numbers have been broken into sets of five. Use letter frequency analysis to crack the code.

09-65-81-92-33   31-40-65-92-68

92-88-88-78-54   92-01-05-09-33

92-81-09-33-92   81-78-40-93-64

01-40-93-31-65   05-31-92-31-01

05-51-64-40-81   43-92-64-73-05

64-92-31-43-43   92-64-73-05-64

65-68-40-93-51   68-78-40-93-33

92-09-43-49-05   64-78-53-09-65

65-53-05-81-68   05-31-78-40-93

53-05-54-65-09   33-92-81-65-68

92-65-78-40-93   64-01-40-59-88

92-31-09-40-31   81-92-33-33-40

59-05-81-68-92   65-43-09-33-88

53-05-92-33-05   43-92-33-81-05

53-53

Puzzle 77

Difficulty Level: Treacherous

XIII-III-VII-II II-III-XI-XII XIX-XXIV

XX-XII-VI-VI-XIX-XXIV-XX

VII-XXIV-XXI-VII-VI-XXII-III-II-XIX-XXIII-XII-I

XIX-XXIV-VI-XII-XI-XI-XIX-XX-XII-XXIV-XVIII-XII VI-III

XXV-XII XXII-XXI-XVI VIII-XII-XII-XXIV

XII-XIV-XXVI-III-XVI-XII-I – XIX I-III-XXIV'VI

V-XXIV-III-XV VIII-XIII XV-XXII-III-XXV.

Puzzle 78

Difficulty Level: Treacherous

09.24.20.24.03 11.20.18 18.12.01.14

11.03.15 01.09.15

13.24.04.15-10.01.11.03.10 24.16 11

26.11.10.24.20 ... 08.14 20.15.07.15.03

04.24.10.17.20.21 10.17.21.09.01 24.16

05.09.17.06.09 09.15 26.11.14

11.07.24.17.18

18.17.10.11.10.01.03.24.12.10

10.09.17.13.05.03.15.06.23.

11.04.08.15.03.01 13.17.23.15,

26.24.03.11.04.10 11.20.18

18.24.21.26.11

Puzzle 79

Difficulty Level: Treacherous

58.70.54.11.82.11.18.54 58.70

05.82.02.21.54.57.38.82.56.21.93.02

58.18 70.57.54

82.11.18.54.82.58.05.54.11.06 54.57

38.57.23.11.82.70.91.11.70.54.18

56.70.06

21.82.57.25.11.18.18.58.57.70.56.20

18.21.58.11.18.

11.23.11.82.02.52.57.06.02

11.70.14.57.02.18 56 18.11.05.82.11.54.

91.56.82.54.58.70 38.56.82.06.70.11.82

Puzzle 80

Difficulty Level: Treacherous

09.20.16.18.15.13.07.16.11,

09.20.16.18.15.13.07.16.11.02, 16.

20.16.02 02.16.11.21.26.22.11.02.13

03.10 07 05.15.11.04 11.04.02

22.02.09.21.02.11.22 20.18 03,

09.20.16.18.15.13.02.13 03.10 04.15.25

11.20 09. 07.25.03.21.20.22.02

03.15.02.21.09.02

Chapter 6

Symbol Substitution Cryptograms

Puzzle 81

Difficulty Level: Easy

⌘ ⧗♍■▬♒   📁♍   ⧗♒💧♎   ♑♎♍♌

📁⧗⌘❄   ❄♍☯♎♒   ❄♍♍✎.

Puzzle 82

Difficulty Level: Easy

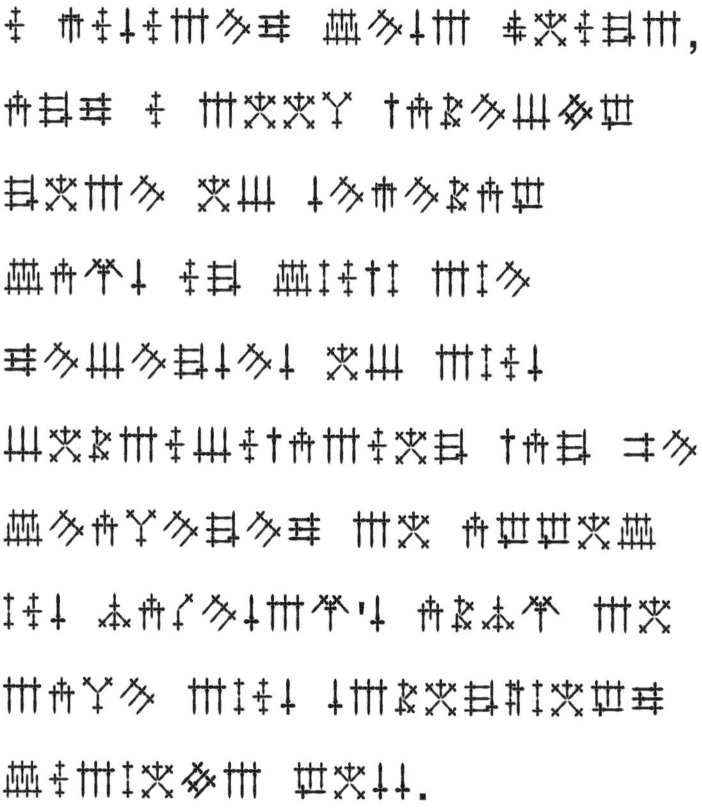

Puzzle 83

Difficulty Level: Easy

Τονιγητ ατ διννερ, υνδερ τηε
ινφλυενχε οφ σομε σπιριτυουσ
λιθυορσ

Puzzle 84

Difficulty Level: Easy

... ▲⚬✖ ✳◆☉▲◎▮⚬ ✎○✖◆

▲⚬ ✖ ✳☉✳◆✳✠☉◆✿

✠✎★✷✖✳▮◆▲☉✎✷

⚬✖ ☆✎✢✿✳ ◆✖✠✖☉○✖.

Puzzle 85

Difficulty Level: Easy

✳❖❋ ★✳❋✳ ✳✧✧❋✳ ❖❖

❋❖✳❋ ❖✦ ❖✳❋ ✳❋❋❋❖❋

❖★✳❖ ❋❋ ✳✧✧❋✳❋✳✳❖❋☆

❋❖ ❋✳★✳ ✳❋✳◉❋ ✳★❖, ✳★☆

❋✳★✳ ✧❖★❖✳✧❖❋. ❖

❋★✳❋✳ ✳❋✳★❋ ❖✦ ❖❖ ✳❖❋

❖❖ ✖◉◉❖★☆ ✳✖❖❋❋❖ ❋★❖

☆◉❋✳❋❋ ✳❖❋ ✧❋★.

Puzzle 86

Difficulty Level: Easy

Puzzle 87

Difficulty Level: Easy

Check out the chart of the Morse code alphabet in Chapter 2.

-... . ... .--. .. - .   - .... .

-... .-. .- .... - .   ..-. .- -.-. .

- .... .- -   .-. .. ... -   --- -.

. ..-. . -. - ...   .. -.

.--. .-. --- .-. .. -... ,   .- ...   ..

-- . - .- .. -.. -.

-... .-. .. . ..-. .-.. -.--

-.. ... .-. .. - --. --- ... .-.

-.-. --- -. .... . .-. ... .- - .. -

--- -. ,   - .... .   .-- .- .-.

-.- --- . ...   -... .- -.. .-.. -- .

Puzzle 88

Difficulty Level: Easy

This is a Passing River cipher. In this cipher some letters share the same symbol, specifically I and Y, O and U, and V and W.

⋊⁊⁊, Ꮛ⋊∼⊓⁊⌡ ⋊ⴸⴸ⊓⋊Ꮒ⊓

ᏋᏋ⋊Ꮒ ⌐⁊Ꮛ⋊⋉⋉⊓

⋊⌐⌡⊓⌐⌡⌒⊓Ꮒ⊓, ∼⊓ ⊿⌐⌐Ꮒ ⁊⌐

∼Ᏼ⋊Ꮒ ⴸ⋊⁊ ⊐⊓ ⁊⌐⁊⊐ Ᏼⴸ

⋊⌡⊐⋊⋊⌡⊐ ⊣⌐⌡ ᏋᏋ⊐ ⁊⊓⊓Ꮒ

ⴸ⌐⁊⊣⌒⊓ⴸᏋ – ⊣⌐⌡ ⋊ ⁊⊓⊓Ꮒ

ⴸ⌐⁊⊣⌒⊓ⴸᏋ ᏋᏋⴸⴸ⊐ ⊿⌐⌡Ꮒ ⊐⊐.

Puzzle 89

Difficulty Level: Easy

...⇂↑⇶∧⌐⇶∧⇊ ⇐☉↳ ⇴⇊∧
⌐⇶∧ ʊ⇧↴ↅ ☉⇧ ⇶⇴↴
⇂↑⇶☉⇴ ⇧ ⌐⇴↴ ⌐⇊↳⇂↑⌐
⇂↑⇧⌐⇶ ⌐⇶⇧⇂↑ ʊ⇧↴ↅ
☉⇧ ⇧↴⇧☉⇊⇴⇴⌐⇧☉↴.
⇧⇧ ⇂↑☉, ⇧ ⇂↑⇧ɕɕ
⇶⇴ʊ∧ ⇴☉⇊∧ ⇂↑↳⌐
⇧↴⇧☉⇊⇴⇴⌐⇧☉↴ ⌐☉
⇂↑⇶⇴⇊∧. ⇧⇧ ↴☉⌐, ⇧
⇂↑⇶ɕɕ ↴∧ʊ∧⇊
⌐☉⇴⇴↳↴⇧⌐⇴⌐∧ ⇂↑⇧⌐⇶
⇐☉↳ ⇴∩⇴⇧↴.

Puzzle 90

Difficulty Level: Easy

e⌂◆⊁≋♌□   ⌘❖□   ◆⊁◆❖□♌

⌘❖□□♌□◆■□♌   ⊁⤢□   ◆♎

◆◆♏❖⌘◆♈   ●○●≋◆⊁⌘□□   ❖◆◆◆

◆○≋♎⌘⤢♈   ○⤢   ○≋⌘⤢◆♏❖⌘

◆◆◆□□⤢♎□♌♌   ⊁⤢□⊁♌,   ⌘❖□⤢□

♌❖○≋◆□   e⌂□   ⤢□◆⊁⌘◆■□◆♈

◆◆⌘⌘◆□   ◆♎⌘□⤢⊙□⤢□♎◆□   ⌘○

○e⌂♌◆≋⤢□   ⌘❖□

♏⤢⊁■◆⌘○□□⌘⤢◆◆   ♌◆♏♎⊁◆.

Puzzle 91

Difficulty Level: Easy

Use the Greek alphabet chart in Chapter 2 for your reference.

...ωηο σερπε ψουρ ενεμιεσ
ωηιλε σερπινγ ιν
ποσιτιονσ οφ τρυστ ιν
Αμεριχαν ιντελλιγενχε ανδ
λαω ενφορχεμεντ.

Puzzle 92

Difficulty Level: Easy

This cipher is written in the Nug-Soth alphabet. C and K, and U and V, share the same symbol.

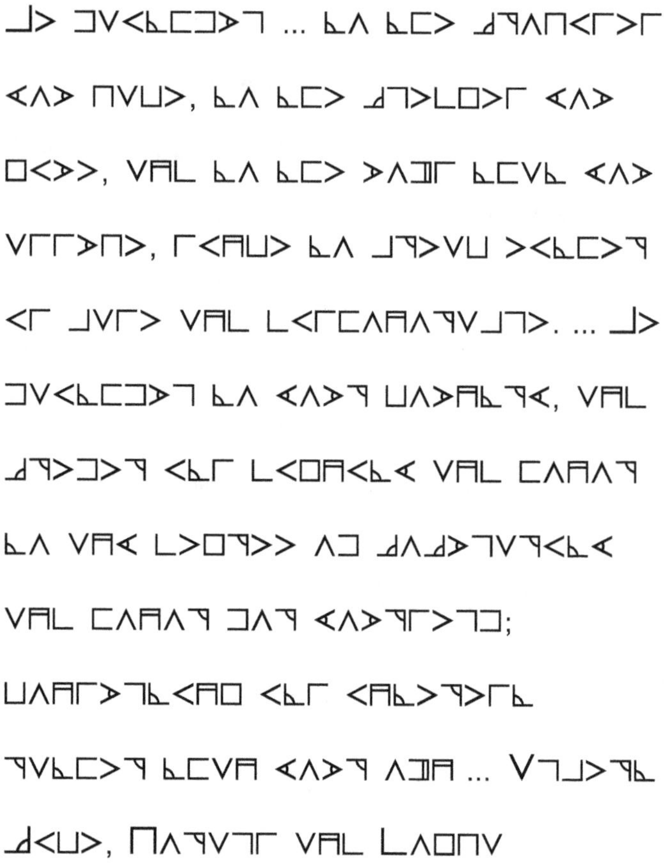

Puzzle 93
Difficulty Level: Tricky

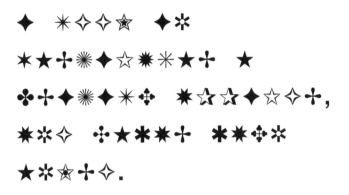

Puzzle 94
Difficulty Level: Tricky

Puzzle 95

Difficulty Level: Tricky

...

Puzzle 96

Difficulty Level: Tricky

This puzzle uses an Illuminati Cipher and has different symbols for uppercase and lowercase letters.

╬ ⌐◲⅊⁊ ⁊⊿⊕⊖⊙⊙⊕⁊⌐

⊕⌐△⊙ ⊕♂ ╬♂⊙ ⌐⊙ ⊕⌐⁊

♀⌐♀♀⊙ ☾♂♀♀⌐⌐⊙⁊

⌐⊖♂⊙⊿⌐ △⁊.

Puzzle 97

Difficulty Level: Tricky

✹✳★✳☆ ✜☆✳✻✧✳★

✧☆✳✳✳✳✳✜ ✻✳✦✳☆✳

★✦☆✳✻ ✦✧ ✜✳✳✳☆✜ ✧✳✳

★✦ ✳✳★ ✻✦✳✳✳, ✳✦

✳✳✻☆✦✻☆✧✜✳✳☆✜

★✧☆✳✳✳✳✻✳✳★ ✳☆ ✳✳★

☆✦☆✳✳✳★✳☆ ✧☆✻✜, ✳✻★☆

✳✦ ✻✧☆★✦✳✧✜★ ✳☆ ✳✳★

☆✦☆✳✳.

Puzzle 98

Difficulty Level: Tricky

.---- . - '...   - .- -.- .   - .... .   -. .- -- .

-.-. .... .- -. --. .   .-   -.-. .. -

....- .-- .-. - .... . .-., .- -. -..

.. -.. . .- - . .... .-.- .-- .. - ....

- .... .   --- .-. .. -.- .. -. .- .-..

.- -- . .-. .. -.-. .- -.

.-. . ....- --- .-.. ..- - .. --- -. .

Puzzle 99

Difficulty Level: Tricky

This is a Passing River cipher. Some letters share the same symbol, specifically I and Y, O and U, and V and W.

⊣ᛁ⅃ ⊏ᴛ⎕ ⌡ᵐᒣ ᛁ⊣ ⊏ᴛ⎕

Ⅴᵑ⁊⊏⅃ᵐ, ᵐ ⊐⎕⌡ ᵑᵐᵒ ⅃ᵢ

⁊ᛁᴛ ᵐ⌡⁊ᛁ⅃⎕ ⊏ᴛᵐ⌡

◁⎕⌡⌡⋈⌡⎓.

Puzzle 100

Difficulty Level: Tricky

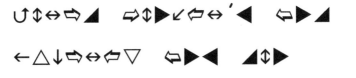

↻↕↔⇨◢ ⇨↕▶↙↩↔'◀ ↩▶◢

←△↓↩↔↩▽ ↩▶◀ ◢↕▶

→↕◀ ⇨ ↩⇨◀◀↩△ ⇨↙↩▽▽

↕← ↩↔↩↻◢. ▽◢▲↓↗↩

↻↓↙↙↓→↩↔

Puzzle 101

Difficulty Level: Tricky

◻ ☆⌂⊡ϙ ⌒◦⋏Ɛ◦'✳ ←

✳φ⌀□φ⌒, △⊡□ ◻◦'✳

ϙ⋏◻✳⇦φ□φƐ

φℓφ□⌔ϙ⋏φ□φ.

ϙ◻φφφ◻Ɛ◐ ⌀⊡⌂◠□φφ

Puzzle 102

Difficulty Level: Tricky

```
-.. . .--. . -.-. - --- .-. ...    .- .-. .

.-.. .. -.- .    --. .-. .- .--. . ... .-.-.-

- ..... .    ..-. .. .-. ... -

.--. .-. . ... ... .. -. --. ...

..-. .-. --- --    - ..... .    .- .-. .

- ..... .    -... . ... - .-.-.-    - ..... .

- ..... .. .-. --    .- -. --.

..-. --- ..- .-. - ....    .-.. .- -.-. --.

-... --- -.. -.-. .-.-.-

-- .- ..- .-. .. -.-. .

--- .-.. -.. .-.. .. . .-.. -..
```

Puzzle 103

Difficulty Level: Treacherous

☆✸ ✧✸☆✿✱✩✿✥✧✩✱※

✱✿☆✪✿✿✸ ✱✿◆✿✱✩✸ ★✿

✩✩✹★✱ ☆✩✱✩✩✩✥✱✿'✸

✩✱✿✸☆✱ ✧✸

✩✩✹✣✱✩☆☆✩✸ ✩✸✥

✩✩✹★✱ ☆✩✱✩✩✩✥✱✿

✣✧✿✱✿✸✩.

Puzzle 104

Difficulty Level: Treacherous

∅∅ ◻ℸ, ▲◠∽∅◻ ▲ઉઉ,
▲♢ ☼◠◻◻∨∅◻ ◻♢
∅◻ℸ ♪▲ℭ∅ℸℭ∞ℬ'ℸ
▲◻♪ℬ, ▲♢ଷ ♢☼
∨☼♪♪☼♢ ℸ→ℬ.

Puzzle 105

Difficulty Level: Treacherous

Puzzle 106

Difficulty Level: Treacherous

This message uses Morse code punctuation as well as letters.

Puzzle 107

Difficulty Level: Treacherous

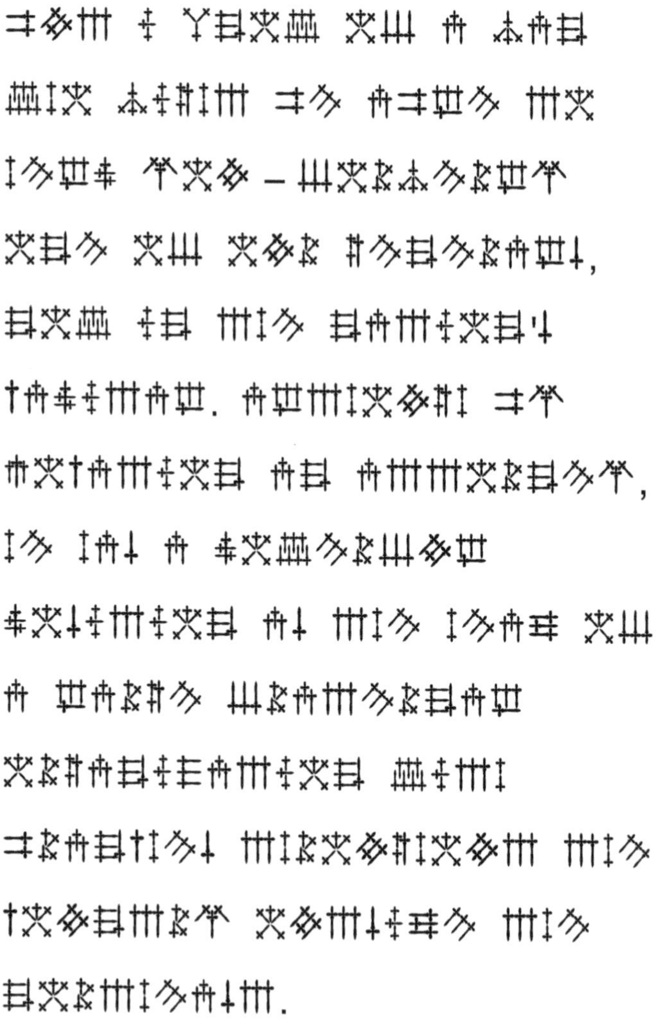

Puzzle 108

Difficulty Level: Treacherous

This puzzle uses an Illuminati Cipher and has different symbols for uppercase and lowercase letters.

Puzzle 109

Difficulty Level: Treacherous

We removed all punctuation and spaces between words in this cipher. The letters are grouped in sets of five. Good luck!

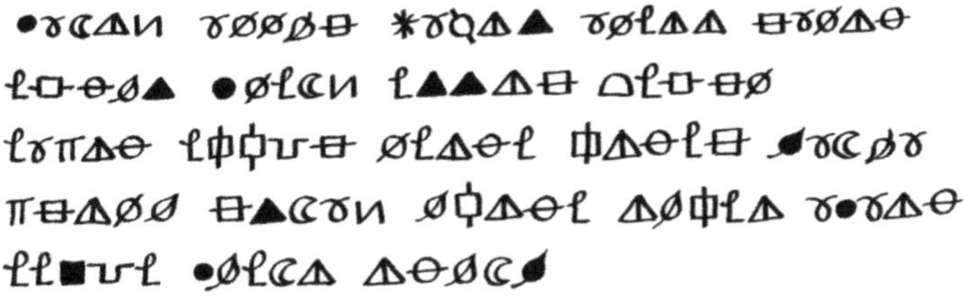

Puzzle 110

Difficulty Level: Treacherous

This is a Passing River cipher. Some letters share the same symbol, specifically I and Y, O and U, and V and W.

Chapter 7
Caesar / Shift Ciphers

Puzzle 111
Difficulty Level: Easy

UIF CSJUJTI BSF OPU UIF POMZ POFT
XJUI TQJFT PO UIF HSPVOE.

Puzzle 112
Difficulty Level: Easy

PDMRU DQGUH LV QRZ FRQYLQFHG
WKDW WKH ZRXOG-EH WUDLWRU LV
ZKR KH VDBV KH LV.

Puzzle 113

Difficulty Level: Easy

MN CNTAS SGHR LDRRZFD VHKK BNLD

SN XNT ZR RNLDSGHMF NE Z

RTQOQHRD.

Puzzle 114

Difficulty Level: Easy

... TJPM YZXDNDJI VWJPO HT

XJHKZINVODJI.

Puzzle 115

Difficulty Level: Easy

... SRI TYPPIH EAEC JVSQ XLI YRMXIH

WXEXIW EPXSKIXLIV MRXS E

FIRIZSPIRX OMRKHSQ SJ MXW SAR.

CSY ERH M GER EGGSQTPMWL KVIEX

XLMRKW.

Puzzle 116

Difficulty Level: Easy

PLRQE ZXOLIFKX'P SLQB CLO

PBZBPPFLK. LMBK TXOCXOB FP LKIV

JLKQEP XTXV.

Puzzle 117

Difficulty Level: Easy

YMJ SJB HTRRFSIJW TK YMJ ZSNTS

KTWHJX, YMFY LJSJWFQ LWFSY, MFX

F KNWR LWFXU TK YMJ HTSHJUY TK

YTYFQ BFW, FSI MJ NX UZWXZNSL

YMFY UTQNHD RTXY ANLTWTZXQD,

STY TSQD IJKJFYNSL ZX TS YMJ KNJQI

TK GFYYQJ, GZY IJXYWTDNSL TZW

HFUFHNYD YT UWTIZHJ JAJS KTTI,

BMJWJAJW MJ HFS.

Puzzle 118

Difficulty Level: Easy

JKP OK. ARAJ ZQNEJC PDA UAWNO KB

PNWRAH PDWP E PKKG EJ AQNKLA, E

GJAS PDWP E SWO BKHHKSAZ,

OKIAKJA BAZANWH JK ZKQXP

OQOLAYPEJC PDWP E DWRA

WYYKILHEYAO, WJZ OAAGEJC PK BEJZ

PDAI.

Puzzle 119

Difficulty Level: Easy

L FDQ WHOO BRX DERXW RQH VXFK
DJHQW. KLV QDPH LV MDVSHU
KDOOLJDQ, DQ DWWRUQHB ZLWK
WKH XQLWHG VWDWHV
GHSDUWPHQW RI VWDWH.

Puzzle 120

Difficulty Level: Easy

COZN ZNK YOTMRK-SOTJKJ
JKJOIGZOUT ZU EUAX VXULKYYOUT
LUX CNOIN EUA NGBK HKIUSK QTUCT
GZ ZNK LHO ...

Puzzle 121

Difficulty Level: Easy

OQTG VJCP CPA QVJGT VKOG KP

JKUVQTA, OCPMKPF HCEGU C

ETQUUTQCFU. QPG RCVJ NGCFU VQ

FGURCKT CPF WVVGT

JQRGNGUUPGUU. VJG QVJGT, VQ

VQVCN GZVKPEVKQP. NGV WU RTCA

YG JCXG VJG YKUFQO VQ EJQQUG

EQTTGEVNA. YQQFA CNNGP

Puzzle 122

Difficulty Level: Easy

CNGZ OY KYVOUTGMK HAZ ZNK BKXE

ZNOTM CK KDKXIOYK JGORE OT UAX

ROBKY? PUNT RK IGXXK,

GZZXOHAZKJ

Puzzle 123

Difficulty Level: Easy

WMS ILMU UFYR AFYPK GQ : Y UYW

MD ECRRGLE RFC YLQUCP WCQ

UGRFMSR FYTGLE YQICB YLW AJCYP

OSCQRGML. YJZCPR AYKSQ

Puzzle 124

Difficulty Level: Easy

GXWB LV WKH PRUDO PDJQHWLVP

ZKLFK FRQWUROV DQG JXLGHV WKH

WUXH PDVRQ'V FRXUVH RYHU WKH

WXPXOWXRXV VHDV RI OLIH. ZKHWKHU

WKH VWDUV RI KRQRU, UHSXWDWLRQ,

DQG UHZDUG GR RU GR QRW VKLQH, ...

WKDW XQHHULQJ PDJQHW VWLOO

VKRZV KLP WKH WUXH FRXUVH WR

VWHHU ... WR SHUIRUP WKDW GXWB,

ZKHWKHU WKH SHUIRUPDQFH EH

UHZDUGHG RU XQUHZDUGHG, LV KLV

VROH FDUH. DQG LW GRWK QRW

PDWWHU, WKRXJK RI WKLV

SHUIRUPDQFH WKHUH PDB EH QR

ZLWQHVVHV, DQG WKRXJK ZKDW KH

GRHV ZLOO EH IRUHYHU XQNQRZQ WR

DOO PDQNLQG. DOEHUW SLNH

Puzzle 125

Difficulty Level: Tricky

LD TYDECFNEPO, T SLGP AWLNPO

XJDPWQ FYOPC L QLWDP YLXP LD L

DPCGTYR XLTO EZ ESP ZQQTNPCD

HTESTY ESP NTCNWP ZQ RPYPCLW

NWTYEZY

Puzzle 126

Difficulty Level: Tricky

... OCVO OCDN JAAZM DN OMPGT

AMJH OCZ KZMNJI RCJNZ IVHZ RVN

NDBIZY VO OCZ WJOOJH JA OCVO

HZNNVBZ.

Puzzle 127

Difficulty Level: Tricky

... KYV DRGJ TRIIP KYV GCRZE

JZXERKLIV FW XVEVIRC SVEVUZTK

RIEFCU. GCVRJV RUMZJV LJ

IVXRIUZEX SFKY DRAFI REUIV REU

XVEVIRC RIEFCU

Puzzle 128

Difficulty Level: Tricky

RO CRKVV WKUO KBBKXQOWOXDC DY

ZED K QBOKD NOKV YP DRO

WKDOBSKV KCCODC YP DRO

MYXPONOBKMI SX IYEB RKXNC.

Puzzle 129

Difficulty Level: Tricky

UBVDEXR FNLM FTDX BM TIITKXGM MH

TEE MATM MAX AXTOBER

TZKBVNEMNKTE BGMXKXLML BG MABL

TKXT – BGVENWBGZ VNUT, ATBMB,

FXQBVH TGW TEE HY VXGMKTE

TFXKBVT – KXJNBKXL MAX XGMKR HY

MAXLX MXKKBMHKBXL BGMH MAX

NGBMXW LMTMXL TL LETOX

MXKKBMHKBXL. HY HNK ETMXK

TFUBMBHGL YHK MATM KXZBHG, RHN

LATEE LTR GHMABGZ MH UBVDEXR.

Puzzle 130

Difficulty Level: Tricky

RD NSYJWRJINFWD XMFQQ XJJ YT NY

YMFY DTZ YFPJ UTXXJXXNTS TK YMJ

QFXY TK YMJ LTQI NRRJINFYJQD.

Puzzle 131

Difficulty Level: Tricky

UKQN UKQJC LNKOLAYP, OLAYEWH

WCAJP IWJJDAEI, SWO LANIEPPAZ PK

HAWZ PDA PAWI PK WNNAOP PDEO

DWHHECWJ BAHHKS WP OPWPA. PDAU

BKQJZ DWHHECWJ ZAWZ, DWREJC

PWGAJ DEO YUWJEZA LEHH.

Puzzle 132
Difficulty Level: Tricky

MBLMIB TEL JXHB EFPQLOV HKLT

KLQEFKD XYLRQ EFPQLOV. VLR ZXK

PBB QEXQ FK QEB PLOQ LC EFPQLOV

QEBV JXHB. D H ZEBPQBOQLK

Puzzle 133
Difficulty Level: Tricky

MABL VHGMKTVM BL LH HGX-LBWXW

MATM B TF LNKIKBLXW MH YBGW BM

PKBMMXG HG UHMA LBWXL HY MAX

ITIXK. EHKW XOXKLAXW

Puzzle 134

Difficulty Level: Tricky

DBEDR SC CEZZBOCCON, XYD DY

ZBYDOMD DRO MYEXDBI PBYW OXOWI

KQOXDC LED DY ZBYDOMD DRO

QYFOBXWOXD YP DRO NKI KQKSXCD

DRO ZOYZVO. BYI RKDDOBCVOI

Puzzle 135

Difficulty Level: Treacherous

NDJ LXAA LXIW PAA SJT WPHIT WPKT

NDJG PVTCIH XC CTL NDGZ RXIN,

QTWXCS QGXIXHW AXCTH, IPZT

UDGBTG VTCTGPA QTCTSXRI PGCDAS

XCID RJHIDSN QN UDGRT, PCS GTIJGC

WXB ID BN RPBE.

Puzzle 136

Difficulty Level: Treacherous

SBE GUR FNXR BS ZL ERCHGNGVBA

NAQ ZL VAABPRAG SNZVYL, PNA JR

ABG XRRC GUVF ORGJRRA

BHEFRYIRF?

Puzzle 137

Difficulty Level: Treacherous

B LATEE FTDX GH XQVATGZX YHK

FTCHK TGWKX NGEXLL BM UX YHK

UXGXWBVM TKGHEW.

Puzzle 138

Difficulty Level: Treacherous

We removed all the spaces and punctuation from this cipher, so you need to use letter frequency analysis.

INBMZ BPMLM IBPWN KTMUM VBDIT

TIVLQ OPIUB PQAXI ABRCV MQTWA

BUGTI ABBMV CWCAT QVSBW GWCZW

ZOIVQ HIBQWV

Puzzle 139

Difficulty Level: Treacherous

This Caesar Cipher has a keyword that will fill in the gap in the message.

B SITUMPQFIT QAU QUMMBOGU

KMUTBRFHUIQ YJS FMU BI: ESFMTBFI

JN F VFPQ _ _ _ _ _ _ _ BI EJGT,

PRFQQUMUT FOJSQ QAU RJSIQMY,

YUQ OUBIE WBQAJSQ QAU HUFIP QJ

PFNUESFMT BQ FTULSFQUGY.

Puzzle 140

Difficulty Level: Treacherous

AOPZ DPSS HSZV OLSW JVCLY AOL

MHJA AOHA CHSSHUKPNOHT YBUZ

HSS VM AOPZ MYVT JHUHKH. THRL

ZBYL OL AOPURZ PA PZ OPZ PKLH.

Puzzle 141

Difficulty Level: Treacherous

As an added twist to this Caesar Cipher, we put all the letters into groups of five.

CRJKE ZXYKZ YRGGV EVUKF SVZEY

VIFEJ KRMVI EZEKY VLGJK RZIJI

FFDNF IBZEX FEDPJ TLCGK LIVFW

KYVYV RUFWK YVTYR DSVIF WTFDD

VITV

Puzzle 142

Difficulty Level: Treacherous

As an added twist to this Caesar Cipher, we removed the spaces between words and all punctuation, and we grouped the letters in sets of five.

KYVVE VDPJJ GZVJS YFYRM VTFDV

KFJGP FELJD LJKSV JFLXY KFLKK

VDGKV UNZKY SIZSV JCVUR NRPRE

UTFDW FIKRS CPYFL JVUKY LJKYV

PNZCC SVTFD VTFEM VIKVU JGZVJ

REURM RZCRS CVWFI FLIJV IMZTV

JLEKQ L

Puzzle 143

Difficulty Level: Treacherous

IE BEDW QI CUD MEHIXYF JXU

SQUIQHI QDT DQFEBUEDI, SQUIQHI

QDT DQFEBUEDI MYBB TKBO QHYIU

QDT CQAU JXUC CYIUHQRBU. QBTEKI

XKNBUO

Puzzle 144

Difficulty Level: Treacherous

As an added twist to this Caesar Cipher, we put all the letters into groups of five.

JRRGP DQQHU VDUHD FROOH FWLRQ

RILQW HOOLJ HQFHH GXFDW LRQWD

VWHDQ GVWBO HPLAH GWRJH WKHUV

RWKDW BRXGR QWQHH GDQBR IWKHV

HWKLQ JVSMR URXUN H

Chapter 8
Masonic Ciphers

Puzzle 145
Difficulty Level: Easy

>□Γ˙ƎV   ˙C⊏

⌐C˙Ǝ⅂□□V⅃>ΓC□

Puzzle 146
Difficulty Level: Easy

⅂Γ˙C⅂□□⊐   VΓ>Π

>ΠC   V<Γ>⅃Π˙□

⅂Γ˙⅃□⅂□˙□□˙>V

Puzzle 147

Difficulty Level: Easy

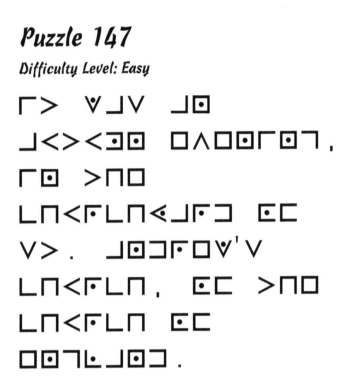

Puzzle 148

Difficulty Level: Easy

This cipher is written in Malachim, a Hebrew-based phonetic alphabet. Some symbols can stand for more than one letter, relating to a phonetic sound rather than a specific letter. For example, the square symbol can be E or O. See Chapter 2 for the full list.

Puzzle 149

Difficulty Level: Easy

Puzzle 150

Difficulty Level: Easy

This puzzle is written in a 19th century French Masonic cipher once used by those who held the 31st degree of initiation in the Scottish Rite, a degree known as "Grand Inquisitor Commander." V and W are encrypted with the same symbol.

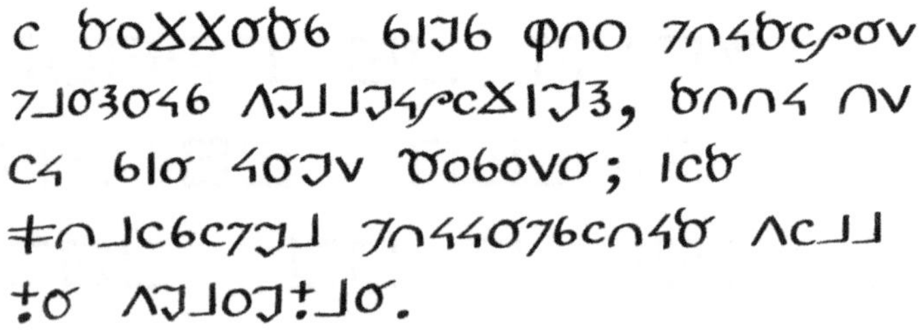

Puzzle 151

Difficulty Level: Easy

This cipher is written in Malachim, a Hebrew-based phonetic alphabet.

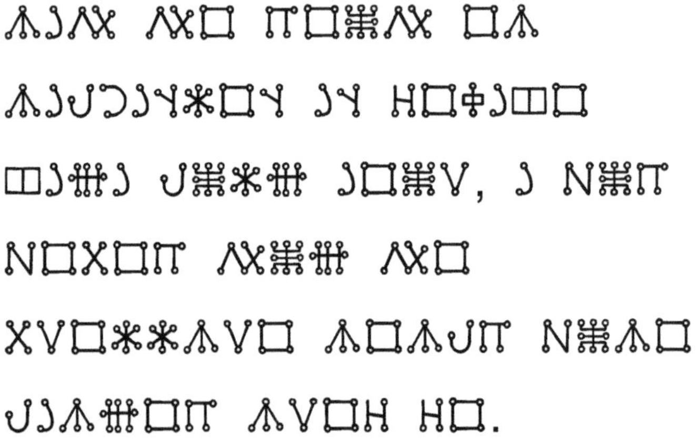

Puzzle 152

Difficulty Level: Easy

>⊓□ ⊡⅃⼂□ ⻤⊏

⻤<⌐ ⼅<⊔⌊⌐⌊

⻤⌐⼅⌐⅃⊡⌐⼂⋀⅃>⌐⊡⊡,

"⼌⊡⌐⼅⼀>⋁ ⻤⊏

>⊓□ ⼅⻤⼂⅃□⊡

⌊⌐⌐⌊⌊⼂□",

⋁⼂⅃⌊⼌⋁ >⻤⻤

⼂<⌊⊓ ⻤⊏ >⊓□

⊔⌐⌐>⌐⋁⊓

⻤⌐⼂□⌐⋁ ⻤⊏

⊡⻤⊔⌐⌊⌐>⼂.

Puzzle 153

Difficulty Level: Easy

This cipher is drawn in Celestial, a phonetic alphabet based on Hebrew. O and U have the same symbol, as do V and W.

ΠΔꟽΠ Δ Ꝏꟽ Ʊ⸜ΔᘒᘒΔᒲ ꟽꟽᒲ
ᓚΔᒲΠ Ꝏ ᒥᒲΔ⸜ᒲ ᒲꟽᒲΔꟽΠ ꟽᒲ ΠᒲΔᓚ
ΠᒲΠ ƱꟽꟽᒲᒲΔᴍΠ ᒲΔᒲᴍ
ꝎꝎ ꟽ ᒪΔᒲᒲ ᴍΠᒲΠ ᒲꟽꟽ ꟽꝎ
ꟽΔ ᒥᴍᒲꝎꟽᒲᴍᒲꟽ ᒲᴍꟽᒲᒲᴍꟽᴍᒲꟽᒲ -
ᒲᴍΠᒲ ᒪΠᒲΠ Δ ᴍꟽᒲ ᒲᒲΔᒲᴍ ΔᒲΠ
ΔꟽΠ ᴍΠᒲΠ ꟽ ꟽΔᒲᴍᒲᒲΔꟽꟽ Ꝏꟽ ᴍᒲΠ
ᒲΔᒲΠᒲ ᘒᒲᴍᘒᒲᒲ.

Puzzle 154

Difficulty Level: Easy

Puzzle 155

Difficulty Level: Easy

Puzzle 156

Difficulty Level: Easy

This puzzle is written in a 19th century French Masonic cipher once used in some chapters of Rose Croix within the Scottish Rite. As is standard in these ciphers based on Hebrew, some letters are encrypted with the same cipher symbol. See Chapter 2 for more detail.

Puzzle 157

Difficulty Level: Easy

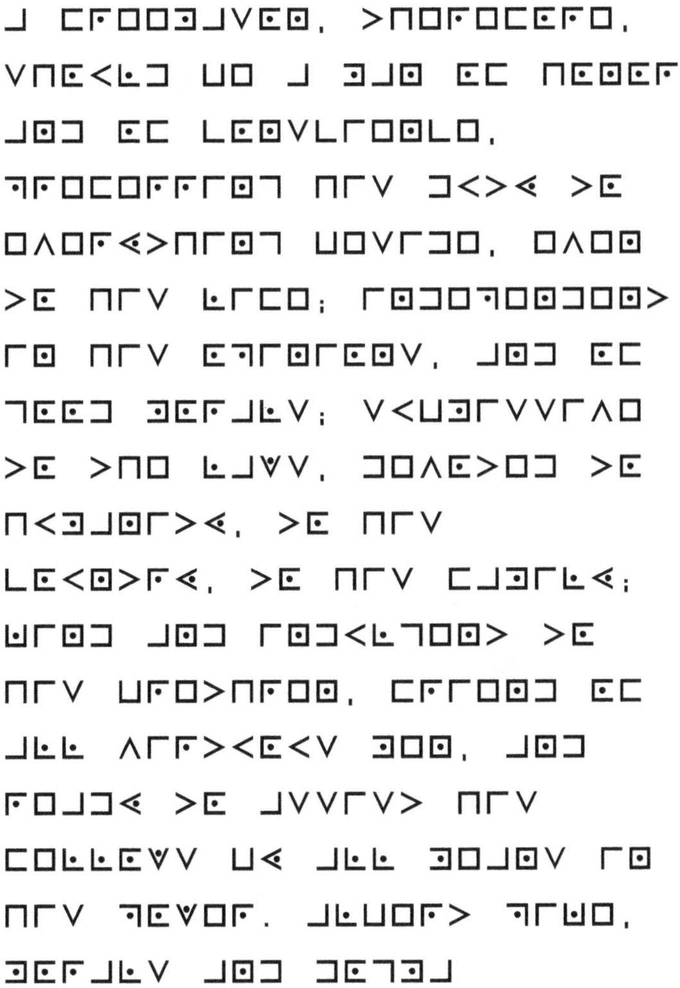

Puzzle 158

Difficulty Level: Tricky

This cipher is written in Malachim, a Hebrew-based phonetic alphabet.

Puzzle 159

Difficulty Level: Tricky

This message is written in the *Cypher of the Rose Croix,* a special Masonic cipher.

Puzzle 160

Difficulty Level: Tricky

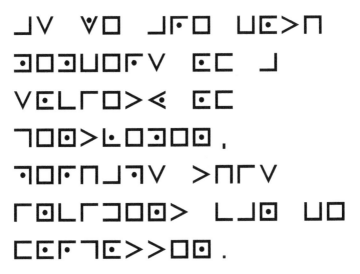

Puzzle 161

Difficulty Level: Tricky

This cipher is in the *Cypher of the Rose Croix.*

Puzzle 162

Difficulty Level: Tricky

This cipher is written in Malachim, a Hebrew-based phonetic alphabet.

Puzzle 163

Difficulty Level: Tricky

This cipher is drawn in Enochian, a phonetic alphabet based on Hebrew. The following letters are encoded as each other: C and K; I and J; U, V, and W.

Puzzle 164

Difficulty Level: Tricky

This puzzle is written in a 19th century French Masonic cipher once used by those who held the 31st degree of initiation in the Scottish Rite, "Grand Inquisitor Commander."

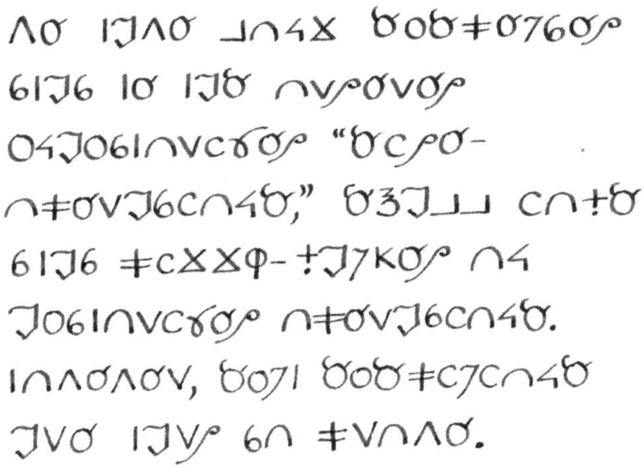

Puzzle 165

Difficulty Level: Tricky

This cipher is in the *Cypher of the Rose Croix.*

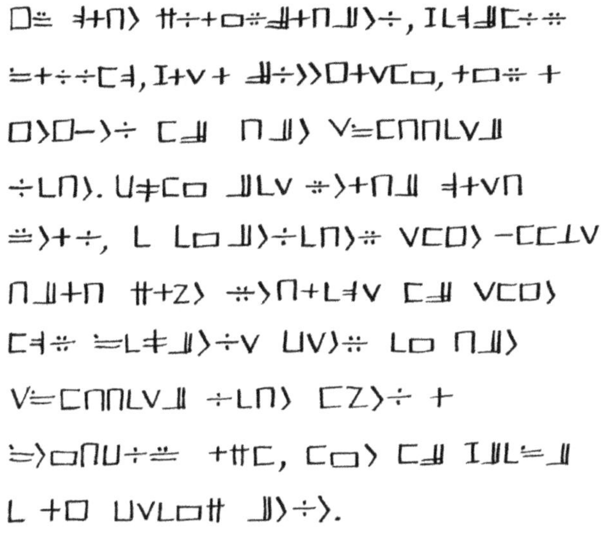

Puzzle 166

Difficulty Level: Tricky

This cipher has a keyword that's a girl's name. See whether you can find it!

Puzzle 167

Difficulty Level: Tricky

>⊓□ ∟⊓⌐□⊏
⊐⌐∨>⌐□∟>⌐⊡□ ⊏⊏
⌐ ⊐⌐ᴸᴸ⊡⊐∟> ⌐∨
>⊓∟> ⊓□ ∟∟⊡ ∨∟<
⊡⊏ ⌐⊡ ∨<∟⊓ ∟
∨∟< >⊓∟> ⌐>
∨⊡<⊡⊐∨ ᴸ⌐ᴸ□
<□∨ .
ᴸ□∨>□⌐ ∪⊏∨ᴸ□∨
ᴸ□∟⌐∨⊏⊡

Puzzle 168

Difficulty Level: Tricky

This cipher is written in Malachim, a phonetic alphabet.

Puzzle 169

Difficulty Level: Treacherous

This cipher has a keyword. See whether you can discover it!

Puzzle 170

Difficulty Level: Treacherous

This cipher has a keyword. See whether you can crack the code!

Puzzle 171

Difficulty Level: Treacherous

ⒽⓋ✱. ▢✿ⓋⓋ▢ⓊⓊ Ɉ✱ ⓨ▢✿
✿Ⓥ✿ɈⓎ▢Ⓟ ✿✱ ✿
▢▢ɅⓋɈ▢Ⓥ. ✿Ⓤ⅄▢ɅⓊⓃ ✿
ɅɈⓅ▢Ʌ, ⅄▢ Ɉ✱ ⓨ▢✿
ⒽɅ▢Ⓝ ▢ⓊⓅ▢Ⓥ Ʌ⅄✿ⓨ ✿
ⓊɈⓋɈ Ⓝ▢Ⓥ✱▢ⓊɅ.

Puzzle 172

Difficulty Level: Treacherous

This cipher is drawn in Enochian, a phonetic alphabet based on Hebrew. The following letters are encoded as each other: C and K; I and J; U, V, and W.

Puzzle 173

Difficulty Level: Treacherous

This cipher has a keyword. See whether you can discover it!

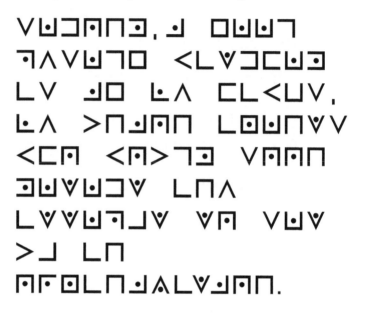

Puzzle 174

Difficulty Level: Treacherous

This cipher is drawn in Celestial, a phonetic alphabet based on Hebrew. O and U have the same symbol, as do V and W.

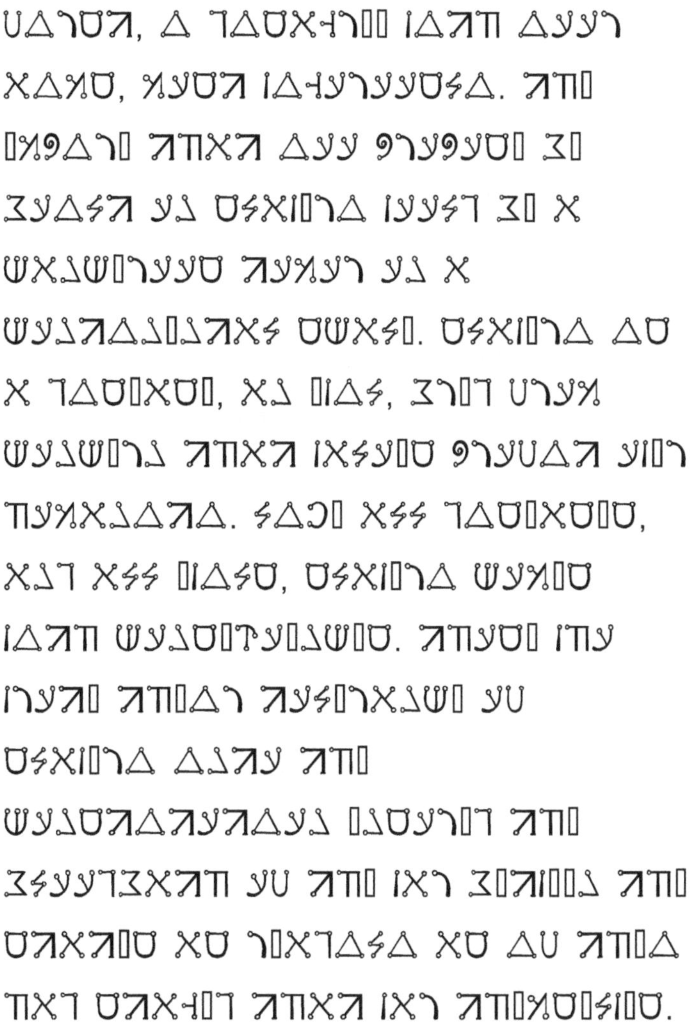

Puzzle 175

Difficulty Level: Treacherous

This puzzle is written in a 19th century French Masonic Scottish Rite cipher used by the Rose Croix chapter of "Macon," possibly a chapter in Mâcon, France. U, V, and W are encoded with the one symbol.

Puzzle 176

Difficulty Level: Treacherous

This cipher is drawn in Celestial, a phonetic alphabet based on Hebrew.

Chapter 9

Rail Fence Ciphers

Puzzle 177

Difficulty Level: Easy

GVSPO TOIMJ SYAMI EUPRT HSAET
SRY

Puzzle 178

Difficulty Level: Easy

AEIAW UDERI OMRCN OLBTA TR

Puzzle 179

Difficulty Level: Easy

CMADR FHCNI ETLRY OCSTE TONOM

NEOTE OTNNA AMFRE AWSPI T

Puzzle 180

Difficulty Level: Easy

YUTRS RACPA LOREM AECET BE

Puzzle 181
Difficulty Level: Easy

TXEOE ERMRI VBOHE ITNEF HINRI

CEUTE ANNII LTHME SCTNC LSMIS EI

Puzzle 182
Difficulty Level: Easy

CGFAH REOTE SNASR O

Puzzle 183
Difficulty Level: Easy

LTHNR HATAE TSOLN IISNI SATRE

ETEOT ESHVI SWLEC TEADT FCOIS

Puzzle 184
Difficulty Level: Easy

BEDAO ELAEH HDEHN NTHPB IFCXT

INDTU CE

Puzzle 185

Difficulty Level: Easy

YUOOK OMIOE EKOAA RMUTB UYUOD

NTNWE HWVRN WFIAO NAOTO X

Puzzle 186

Difficulty Level: Easy

TEAIA NEOEN ISOTN SHMNL EVLPA

DTCNE TZ

Puzzle 187

Difficulty Level: Easy

DPOAY YNISA ELVRE FRILM CLIGN

TTOIE HROD

Puzzle 188

Difficulty Level: Tricky

AER LC CRO LIAL

Puzzle 189
Difficulty Level: Tricky

VEFND SAGEO AITOP ASNMP RLTNT

WSPIT RYLAA EIOTN

Puzzle 190
Difficulty Level: Tricky

GVMLV TMCUI CALSI EYOEO YOSNH

REX

Puzzle 191
Difficulty Level: Tricky

TSLNN NHSEA LACEE OFTIA THFNE

HXCLC SSITT I

Puzzle 192
Difficulty Level: Tricky

HWODF OIITC NATEF EALHS YASOG

OOYUT SOOTC MATRL TEEER X

Puzzle 193
Difficulty Level: Tricky

CTEEE CGRHV DSHEH MTDRH AIAIH

OKTRH ANIMA SAGEA OROTM RNNTW

IGOGL AGAIE NNOFE KSNUL HD

Puzzle 194
Difficulty Level: Tricky

DTSTO NFMLV PYACE OOPEE THCNE

TOTEA IANEO EOORS OITSX NRNET

SHNEL TUSAX

Puzzle 195
Difficulty Level: Tricky

YUABA SRDHT ORPLC TOFRH CAILE

IEEPD TOSRA MNOMY ESUET AYUAP

IAINO TEIWL BGVNX EIIUT ETET

Puzzle 196
Difficulty Level: Tricky

TMAII PFYSE TTEDY RHTAI HSESG

WLDSP ERRMO RCENI HNESC NSFOR

ECIGH LSLNX ISELA AOURW INOOU

ANETE

Puzzle 197
Difficulty Level: Tricky

GLNOA CHMHY METEE DNTED AHTES

ALERS ISNNM OREOR INTO

Puzzle 198
Difficulty Level: Tricky

AIGWH CEGBD NHSAA THTEI EBAUE

EERSX ACMSM AIHPL CNTOO GRAHW

RIECO AYRNA

Puzzle 199

Difficulty Level: Treacherous

HEIYN AESLS MCETS VWTBH DRDIL

EAEEA

Puzzle 200

Difficulty Level: Treacherous

IEOAR ESAPA TYUSB OHRAO XPLOA

TMN

Puzzle 201
Difficulty Level: Treacherous

TSEHH TNETT EMENE MEORI AEVRA

HOHGE CR

Puzzle 202
Difficulty Level: Treacherous

AWETE RTDLH EMTCT RMTUF HEEXT

GNRIE HEAAE OEFRX HUEEE PAHIS

SNCNA YOVXT NOOC

Puzzle 203

Difficulty Level: Treacherous

SSENO RTEFE TUYON WITCT HINHR

AFITD HHARL MOIHH STSTI IAIAL

AWTEI EETEI ESSII C

Puzzle 204

Difficulty Level: Treacherous

EMOFA CXEYJ HEORL ITDCG MRNRR

EBDAL HNAOA DGNEE ROAJN ENN

Puzzle 205

Difficulty Level: Treacherous

AELWE ONAEL LRLIO AHNGO IGMSF

RXITE EONNT IADHT OJFSN TBNDS

THEO (4-rail)

Puzzle 206

Difficulty Level: Treacherous

IPOAN TAHSR MRHTA OIHMN RAOEU

SWECN WTADA TTARB TLEEO HMAEE

DUSDE L (5-rail).

Puzzle 207

Difficulty Level: Treacherous

SILTI NEULR SOHNP ENIMN EMRAO

SELTU IRIMT GNAAS OGHEA NITTT

ETDAL EUSCW NXOHH E (4-rail)

Chapter 10

Keyboard Codes

Puzzle 208

Difficulty Level: Easy

86 9428 343
4 2667273
437 232889

Puzzle 209

Difficulty Level: Easy

Puzzle 210

Difficulty Level: Easy

43g7i3e g6 g95y D9ht43ww qhe T3h34qo

@qwy8ht59h

Puzzle 211

Difficulty Level: Easy

O s, siyjptoxrf yp ,slr upi s goms; pggrt

pg 3-.--- [pimfd/

Puzzle 212

Difficulty Level: Easy

shoysyomh gpt S,rtovsm rc[smdopm

omyp yjr Hp;frm Votv;r pg s 2.--- ,o;r

tsfoid. vrmyrtrf pm Jsbsms/

Puzzle 213

Difficulty Level: Easy

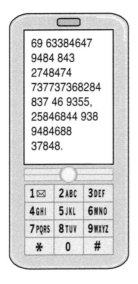

```
69 63384647
9484 843
2748474
737737368284
837 46 9355,
25846844 938
9484688
37848.
```

Puzzle 214

Difficulty Level: Easy

y3q45 59 w33 5y3 9009457h8583w 5yq5

5y8w d9h58h3h5 9rr34w 59 j3h 9r f8w89h

qhe w543ht5y 9r 28ool

Puzzle 215

Difficulty Level: Easy

Puzzle 216

Difficulty Level: Easy

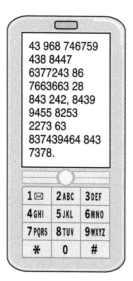

Puzzle 217

Difficulty Level: Easy

```
4693837, 4'83
73236859
232663 29273
63 843 9675 63
7663663 9466
968 64448
3463 63
46837378.
```

```
1 ⊠    2 ABC   3 DEF
4 GHI  5 JKL   6 MNO
7 PQRS 8 TUV   9 WXYZ
*      0       #
```

Puzzle 218

Difficulty Level: Easy

```
36287464 66
638872549464
843 3336787
63 843
3636437 63
843 628466 86
779 66
2637422.
```

```
1 ⊠    2 ABC   3 DEF
4 GHI  5 JKL   6 MNO
7 PQRS 8 TUV   9 WXYZ
*      0       #
```

Puzzle 219

Difficulty Level: Easy

)J4 T9JWP 69- 60 54H4PE{ WP3W7E

UWG4 W E4F0JR

-50T4EE90J 9J 54E45G4. J9Y4P

J9F0PE0J

Puzzle 220

Difficulty Level: Tricky

;ry d;o[yjsy jod vjorg pg d[ord. <skpt

Kpjm Smftr. epi;f nr ,rryomh eoyj s

er;;=[;svrf ytsoypt kidy dpiyj pg Erdy

{pomy. pm Dr[yr,nrt 32dy/

Puzzle 221

Difficulty Level: Tricky

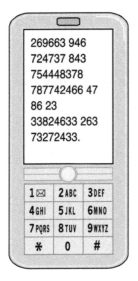

```
269663 946
724737 843
754448378
787742466 47
86 23
33824633 263
73272433.
```

Puzzle 222

Difficulty Level: Tricky

```
743 423 66
7278 46 269
63 8447
```

Puzzle 223

Difficulty Level: Tricky

```
46646368
927
2389336
66784 263
76884
```

1 ✉	2 ABC	3 DEF
4 GHI	5 JKL	6 MNO
7 PQRS	8 TUV	9 WXYZ
*	0	#

Puzzle 224

Difficulty Level: Tricky

I[o fkd'' kdnt [oy houoyt p, i[oy kd,gf/

jodyg pu rt''#

Puzzle 225

Difficulty Level: Tricky

```
4 6878 5665
24323 86 843
8379 7325
76774245489
8428 93 74255
668 7738245 -
668 8447 8463,
28 53278.
```

Puzzle 226

Difficulty Level: Tricky

Fojjtfu i[o b[,fpgty Moyi[, >d,,ktp./

boyyt,u'i du HMP <dup[,d' Ftboypui

Gpnpfp[, _kpytg 37 Lo,t 3-99+/ .di mt [oy

;p,g [h []tydupnt

Puzzle 227

Difficulty Level: Tricky

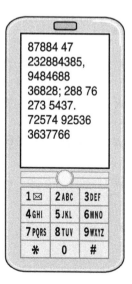

```
9687
467847437
273 843 6275
63 26
46337363368,
732724464
6463.
```

Puzzle 228

Difficulty Level: Tricky

```
87884 47
232884385,
9484688
36828; 288 76
273 5437.
72574 92536
3637766
```

Puzzle 229

Difficulty Level: Tricky

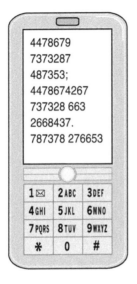

4478679
7373287
487353;
4478674267
737328 663
2668437.
787378 276653

Puzzle 230

Difficulty Level: Treacherous

&08 kw7 54fwpp u03 w k454 h07 3we u8jy

we w e-7 9j 7085 fwk- e0k4 69k4 wy0;

^u4 k4k057 0t Jw6uwj Uwp4 9e e69pp

h59yu6 wk0jy k7 k4j;

Puzzle 231

Difficulty Level: Treacherous

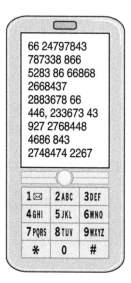

Puzzle 232

Difficulty Level: Treacherous

Puzzle 233

Difficulty Level: Treacherous

Aworwnvwe 29m `76`

Puzzle 234

Difficulty Level: Treacherous

Look out, the keyboard shift changes from one system to another somewhere within this code!

trfotrvy pmr pt ,ptr pg yjr LHJ=26

dsyr;;oyrd imfrt upit vpmytp; yp fp dp,r

wiovl dvsmd pg yjr strsd votv;rf pm yjr

syysvjrf ,s[/ Yjr htsboyp,rytov

vs[sno;oyord pg yjr LHJ=26d djpi;f s;;pe

upi yp e353d5 e8w574gqhd3w 8h 5y3

#q45y[w t4qf85q589hqo r83oe 5yq5

d97oe g3 qww9d8q53e 285y oq4t3

qj97h5w 9r q y3qf6 j35qok o8i3 43r8h3e

t9oel Qhe 63wk 5y343 8w 5yq5 j7dyl

Puzzle 235

Difficulty Level: Treacherous

```
5437 273 5453
24453736:
8439'73 4273
9675, 288 48'7
96784 48
2322873 843
388873 3373637
66 8436. 726
32847
```

1 ✉	2 ABC	3 DEF
4 GHI	5 JKL	6 MNO
7 PQRS	8 TUV	9 WXYZ
*	0	#

Chapter 11

Assorted Ciphers

* *

*1*n this chapter we include the following ciphers for you to solve:

- ✔ Atbash Ciphers
- ✔ Caesar Box Ciphers
- ✔ Columnar Transposition Ciphers
- ✔ Newspaper Codes
- ✔ Twisted Path Box Ciphers

Chapter 2 tells you how to solve each of these puzzle types.

 Grab a notebook or scrap paper before you start working on the puzzles in this chapter! You'll need the space to sketch out boxes, columns, coded alphabets, and so on.

Puzzle 236

Difficulty Level: Easy

This is an Atbash Cipher.

NZQLI ZMWIV RH HSLXPVW. GSRH RH ZM LUUVI LU
GIVZHLM UILN Z NZQLI URTFIV DRGSRM GSV ZINB LU GSV
XLOLMRHGH, URTSGRMT ZTZRMHG GSV YIRGRHS XILDM!

Puzzle 237
Difficulty Level: Easy

It is impossible to give any full account of Machiavelli's official duties. He wrote many thousands of despatches and official letters, which are still preserved. He was on constant errands of State through the Florentine dominions. But his diplomatic missions and what he learned by them make the main interest of his office ... the opportunities to the Secretary of learning men and things, intrigue and policy, the Court and the gutter were invaluable.

At the camp of Caesar Borgia, in 1502, he found in his host that fantastic hero whom he incarnated in The Prince, and he was practically an eye-witness of the amazing masterpiece, the Massacre of Sinigaglia.

Introduction by Henry Cust
to Machiavelli's *The Art of War* and *The Prince*

Puzzle 238

Difficulty Level: Easy

This is a Caesar Box Cipher.

MAXEIIM YRTTNPE PEEOEHS LTNOIES AOSUNRA NOITAEG
SEVLCDE

Puzzle 239

Difficulty Level: Easy

This is an Atbash Cipher.

OVHHLM GL GSV NLWVIM VCVXFGREV : ZODZBH SZMT LM
GL BLFI IVXVRKGH!

Puzzle 240

Difficulty Level: Easy

This is a Caesar Box Cipher.

OTEEKON FURHNLO TACEOUT HLIMWTH EIRUAEI ANCSBLN
CNLTSYG

Puzzle 241

Difficulty Level: Easy

This is an Atbash Cipher.

R ZTIVV DRGS BLF: DZGXS DROPRMHLM. SV RH MLG
VMGRIVOB GL YV GIFHGVW. SLDVEVI, SRH LMTLRMT
ZHHLXRZGRLMH RM NZWIRW ZMW NVCRXL XRGB NZB YV
FHVUFO GL FH.

Puzzle 242
Difficulty Level: Easy

The urge to discover secrets is deeply ingrained in human nature; even the least curious mind is roused by the promise of sharing knowledge withheld from others. Some are fortunate enough to find a job which consists in the solution of mysteries, whether it be the physicist who tracks down a hitherto unknown nuclear particle or the policeman who detects a criminal. But most of us are driven to sublimate this urge by the solving of artificial puzzles devised for our entertainment. Detective stories or crossword puzzles cater for the majority; the solution of secret codes may be the hobby of a few.

The Decipherment of Linear B
John Chadwick
(Cambridge University Press, 1958)

Puzzle 243
Difficulty Level: Easy
This is a Caesar Box Cipher.

WKCHEPORC INOEREUET LOUMECHCI KWRUVTATO
ISSSETVCN NMETNHEOT SEBNSAANO OOUEUTDNM
NFTVSYIEE

Puzzle 244

Difficulty Level: Easy

This is an Atbash Cipher.

R HGILMTOB IVXLNNVMW GSZG BLF ZKKOB ULI Z
KLHRGRLM DRGSRM GSV XVMGIZO RMGVOORTVMXV
ZTVMXB, DRGSRM GSV WRIVXGLIZGV LU LKVIZGRLMH.
(GSZG DLFOW YV GSV HKRVH.)

Puzzle 245

Difficulty Level: Easy

This is an Atbash Cipher.

HLIIB GL YV LFG LU GLFXS ULI HL OLMT. ZH R ZKKILZXS
IVGRIVNVMG, GSV LKKLIGFMRGB GL HSZIV RMULINZGRLM
DRGS BLF SZH YVVM WRNRMRHSRMT ULI HLNV GRNV.

Puzzle 246

Difficulty Level: Easy

This is a Caesar Box Cipher drawn in a rectangle.

IKAAOMOABE FCPNUTNTLR YRHSRHTYEN OYYWPEKOME
UPIERNNUIU TTSROYORSM HOTTBOWPPA IGHOLUWREN
NREYEDHOTN

Puzzle 247

Difficulty Level: Easy

This is an Atbash Cipher.

RM XBYVIHKZXV VEVIBLMV DROO YV ZMLMBNLFH ULI
URUGVVM NRMFGVH. TIZSZN TIVVMOVZU

Puzzle 248

Difficulty Level: Tricky

This is a Caesar Box Cipher.

OHRHHHNS UAMOIIEE TTEULASV SQESAOUE IUTEDNMN
DAIIEEMI EKNNLFEN TEGPPIRG

Puzzle 249

Difficulty Level: Tricky

This is a Caesar Box Cipher drawn in a rectangle.

GAOCTNDR ELLIOGES NADDCESU ERDEHSFR RNESAIOE

Puzzle 250

Difficulty Level: Tricky

This is a Caesar Box Cipher.

TEYET HNOTO ETFRR IITAX DTHIY

Puzzle 251

Difficulty Level: Tricky

This is a Caesar Box Cipher drawn in a rectangle.

TRUNONE HKTTTFS EEUAHOT DNSFERE ASAEUCR YATLNED
DBLLISA AOATOYY

Puzzle 252

Difficulty Level: Tricky

This is a Twisted Path Box Cipher, with a down-and-up path.

TDEIMFOGRX HLNSPERRON AOCSLBAEUO TGIIYTNHPI
DARENSOTOS RECROUTOFI ENLITMHNMV AIEPTTEAEH
MMOMOIRENT OFFEBEAGWI

Puzzle 253

Difficulty Level: Tricky

This is a Twisted Path Box Cipher, with a clockwise spiral path.

OARLINGTONNOW TSAREONTHESTR KEHTMYSELFLOE
CVGEDPIKESMOE AIUVTINGNEEKT BTAEIDPOLASSS
LCCIALEMIRSLL LEYRWARECTAIO ATLTEREWEHGKO
FERREERTEEEK EDAENSAWTUBPI WSEHTOLCNIALN
TSEGGUSEMROFG

Puzzle 254

Difficulty Level: Tricky

This is a Twisted Path Box Cipher, with an up-and-down path.

ATTCECOTMR TSDESNRSAM EDALAAEANY SETLTLDRNL
ITAOELIAHT TIOCLIRFEN SNVDLEEOIE EUENIVCSMC
LERATRTTWE FHTSEUSNER

Puzzle 255

Difficulty Level: Tricky

This is a Caesar Box Cipher drawn in a rectangle.

FEENTTYHDN EMDYHHCEBT WOTIAEORRH FRHNNYUTEE
AEETTOLHAC LFMEHNDAKO SIILELITDD ERNLOYNNAE
IMDINTVOVB DLSGEREOIR EYOETINNDE AGFNHETEKA
SRSTADACAK HIOMTTCOHE APMEIHIUNR VPANFEPLIS

Puzzle 256

Difficulty Level: Tricky

This is a Caesar Box Cipher of a quote by Jerome K. Jerome.

ISOLHCAPG TTLLUORTO IHITNUEIO SECHLRAOD
ABYEESNNL LETTSEEAI WSORSYXLA ATTUOOCLR
YPETFUEYX

Puzzle 257

Difficulty Level: Tricky

Can you discover what work Tu Mu is commenting on here?

Your ... spy must be a man of keen intellect, though in outward appearance a fool; of shabby exterior, but with a will of iron. He must be active, robust, endowed with physical strength and courage: thoroughly accustomed to all sorts of dirty work, able to endure hunger and cold, and to put up with shame and ignominy. Tu Mu

Puzzle 258

Difficulty Level: Treacherous

This is a Twisted Path Box Cipher, with a counterclockwise spiral path.

NARRAOT GFEGNAH EODNAHS ARRERCI NMAJOXW OTHEREI

Puzzle 259

Difficulty Level: Treacherous

This is a Twisted Path Box Cipher, with an up-and-down path.

MOISEF ETGOSO ANNNSR TOOEIP AIFVOE LTRANU LIEGAR XNCELT YGOHSA

Puzzle 260

Difficulty Level: Treacherous
This is a Twisted Path Box Cipher, with a down-and-up path.

ISFDHYSUL WIRRITSVT RHOASSHEU ITMOMEIHR TEABAJPTE

Puzzle 261

Difficulty Level: Treacherous
This is a Columnar Transposition Cipher. The keyword is WILDCAT. (Chapter 2 has instructions on how to solve this cipher.)

YLPIMSS WTUTOAE DGNKIOL REHNTOW APODTTA ILTIONR HTISWAE TEKASOB TIUFRUF HWRDEIN CEHHSAC HDERIER EHPCIRR SSEDMAE OYOETUG

Puzzle 262

Difficulty Level: Treacherous
This is a Twisted Path Box Cipher, with a down-and-up path.

DILWEEHHTI CNOHLRTEDM BHTOPIENEU AISPOTHARS DSIUEWWNET NUPTPAYDDC ANDTRSAWNO HKEHUODOON GNDAONONWF NOATYETDIE IWOLFORESS

Puzzle 263

Difficulty Level: Treacherous
This is a Twisted Path Box Cipher, with a counterclockwise path.

RERUTCIP EAAPERPR LSRREMDE AWEGEBEG TETOSUSR IDISCUSA VETOTHEL

Puzzle 264

Difficulty Level: Treacherous

This is a Columnar Transposition Cipher. The keyword is ZIRCON. (Chapter 2 has instructions on how to solve this cipher.)

HNOETI EYISYR UWDLOT OESSPB EBOFLI ETCSHR ITHSTO
EIJSTR AOEFST RUTDAG SEESAH FSHTOT DOOCLE DFREEN
HCWOYA RVHTEE ISLLWI HOPATN FERONP RWAEOT SOYXNS

Puzzle 265

Difficulty Level: Treacherous

This is a Twisted Path Box Cipher, with a diagonal path.

AAMOFESENG SARFREDTOE TEAPNNOTTA TCETERLHSN
TRAPGAEEDN INEANRCIIT IDNOWINSEN NIIIFTTROA
ZTTFESNILZ AHOREATLYY

Puzzle 266

Difficulty Level: Treacherous

This is a Caesar Box Cipher.

HEEEAOLHNG EIMCNOADDW TTAODRCICO RHSUHSKSOD
UEFLEPITNE SRADWINATH TORSATGNRO EFAPSTBCOU
DTSIAEOELS NHHTPRTAPE

Puzzle 267

Difficulty Level: Treacherous

This is a Twisted Path Box Cipher, with a diagonal path.

PTAREAS ULUGBKT LOGEEHH YSNTCAT IOATTEM NNABKTI
DWASWAN

Chapter 12

Anagrams and Cryptic Clues

- -

Easy

Puzzle 268
Anagram: FEATHERBRAIN TIN GHOST (2, 5, 3, 3, 7)

Puzzle 269
Anagram: I'm not interested in preserving the status quo; I want to THRIVE TO ROW (9, 2). —*Niccolo Machiavelli*

Puzzle 270
Cryptic Clue: Countenance an unruly café (4)

Puzzle 271
Anagram: CHANCY PRESTIGE BISON (3, 10, 6)

Puzzle 272
Anagram: Freedom of the press is guaranteed only to SOOTHE NEON WHOW (5, 3, 3, 3). —*A. J. Liebling*

Puzzle 273
Cryptic Clue: Palm tree rendezvous (4)

Puzzle 274
Anagram: Get your facts first, and then you can SMOTHER DITT (7, 4) as much as you please. —*Mark Twain*

Puzzle 275
Cryptic clue: Higher great lake (8)

Puzzle 276
Anagram: Immorality: the morality of those who are
ATTENTIVE HERB MAGI (6, 1, 6, 4). —*Henry Lewis Mencken*

Puzzle 277
Anagram: SAD SEA RIVER (11)

Puzzle 278
Cryptic Clue: Chickens can be found in Athens (4)

Puzzle 279
Cryptic Clue: It's untrue fleas get confused (5)

Puzzle 280
Anagram: A + B + C = Success if, A = Hard Work, B = Hard Play,
C = KEY IMPETUOUS HUG NORTH (7, 4, 5, 4). —*Albert Einstein*

Puzzle 281
Anagram: CLERIC LENGOD (6, 6)

Puzzle 282
Cryptic Clue: Exercise the locomotive (5)

Puzzle 283
Anagram: And Joseph . . . said unto them, SOUP ER ISAEY (3,
3, 5); you have come to observe the ESSAEKNEWS (10) of the
country. —*Genesis 42:9, modern translation*

Puzzle 284
Cryptic Clue: Lure held by a bonafide coyote (5)

Puzzle 285
Anagram: HERITAGE TRUMP MEN (6, 10)

Puzzle 286
Anagram: TROPHY GYP CAR (12)

Puzzle 287
Anagram: GET HOLD (3, 4)

Puzzle 288
Cryptic Clue: Cooked yam for a month? (3)

Puzzle 289
Cryptic Clue: Fish in fortunate places (4)

Puzzle 290
Anagram: Be kind, for everyone you meet is fighting BALD HATE RAT (1, 4, 6). —*Plato*

Puzzle 291
Anagram: UNWORO (3, 3)

Puzzle 292
Cryptic Clue: Gable mangled a bread roll (5)

Puzzle 293
Anagram: Friends come and go, but enemies CULMAUCETA (10). —*Henry David Thoreau*

Puzzle 294
Anagram: BUDGET ALONE (6, 5)

Puzzle 295
Cryptic Clue: Nocturnal mammal hit the ball (3)

Tricky

Puzzle 296
Cryptic Clue: Annoyed crucifix (5)

Puzzle 297
Anagram: EDIBLE DOVE WAFER (4, 7, 4)

Puzzle 298
Cryptic Clue: Ceremonies among the broken tiers (5)

Puzzle 299
Anagram: When cryptography TULIOSA DEW (2, 8), bayl bhgynjf jvyy unir cevinpl. —*Anonymous*

Puzzle 300
Anagram: Do not regret growing old; many are IDLE EIGHTEEN PRIVED (6, 3, 9). —*Ogden Nash*

Puzzle 301
Anagram: Scratch a lover, and OFFENDIA (4, 1, 3). —*Dorothy Parker*

Puzzle 302
Cryptic clue: Don't be scared by an unruly oat fern (4, 3)

Puzzle 303
Anagram: The only way to make a man trustworthy MUST RIOT THIS (2, 2, 5, 3). —*Henry L. Stimson*

Puzzle 304
Cryptic Clue: Drink can be a part of acid erosion (5)

Puzzle 305
Anagram: UTMOST FINAL (4, 3, 4)

Puzzle 306
Cryptic Clue: Pairs jostling to get to the French capital (5)

Puzzle 307
Cryptic Clue: Long gun in humus ketchup (6)

Puzzle 308
Anagram: SPECTRA EEKE (4, 1, 6)

Puzzle 309
Cryptic Clue: Found in Hamburg undying? A nice red! (8)

Puzzle 310

Anagram: In 1765, Parliament passed the Stamp Act, which, as any American high school student can tell you, was an act that apparently HASN'T ADMITTED HOG SWIM PHOTO (3, 9, 2, 2, 4, 6). —*Dave Barry*

Puzzle 311

Cryptic Clue: Upright newspaper article (6)

Puzzle 312

Anagram: Good advice is always certain to be ignored, but START NOVITIATE SONG HEN TOO (5, 2, 6, 3, 2, 4, 2). — *Agatha Christie*

Puzzle 313

Anagram: OKLUG LOUTDLACOS (4, 4, 2, 2, 3)

Puzzle 314

Anagram: The hottest places in hell are reserved for those who, in time of great moral crisis, ANNIHILATE TERRY TITANIUM (8, 5, 10). —*Dante*

Puzzle 315

Cryptic Clue: Widespread army commander (7)

Puzzle 316

Cryptic Clue: Agitated magnate turns red (7)

Puzzle 317

Anagram: SETTLE STRATOSPHERE YIELD (6, 7, 4, 6)

Treacherous

Puzzle 318

Cryptic Clue: Citrus pies reveal agents (5)

Puzzle 319

Cryptic Clue: Reside in a Masonic group (5)

Puzzle 320
Anagram: NIGHT SMOKE LOON (7, 3, 4)

Puzzle 321
Anagram: I think it will be a clash between the political will and the MAIDSERVANT TWITION (14, 4). —*Lynn and Jay, "Yes Minister"*

Puzzle 322
Cryptic Clue: A broken tablet leads to armed conflict! (6)

Puzzle 323
Cryptic Clue: Damaged ragged blade (6)

Puzzle 324
Anagram: We'd all like to vote for the best man but SAD EVE HAD NECTARINE (3, 5, 1, 9). —*Kin Hubbard*

Puzzle 325
Anagram: Absolute Power, once in fear for the safety of its tenure, TUB CUT REBEL CANON (6, 3, 2, 5). —*Albert Pike, Morals and Dogma*

Puzzle 326
Cryptic Clue: Some da Vinci pheromones hold a code (6)

Puzzle 327
Anagram: When I heard the words ROMANTIC VIGILANTE IS IN (8, 13) my mindset changed considerably. —*Oliver North*

Puzzle 328
Cryptic Clue: Grated Edam cheese makes a good drink! (4)

Puzzle 329
Cryptic Clue: Elite sports group alliance (6)

Puzzle 330
Anagram: I'm proud of the fact that I never DETEST OLIVINE PLAN KNOW (8, 7, 2, 4). —*Thomas A. Edison*

Puzzle 331

Cryptic Clue: Broken, worn key to the big city (3,4)

Puzzle 332

Anagram: Knowledge of the enemy's dispositions can only be obtained MRFETHER MOON (4, 5, 3). —*Sun Tzu, "The Art of War"*

Puzzle 333

Anagram: SECLUDE HIS TIN MIT (4, 1, 4, 7)

Puzzle 334

Cryptic Clue: Shelter can be found by upsetting Hades (5)

Puzzle 335

Anagram: It is double pleasure COERCIVE DEED TEETHIVE (2, 7, 3, 8). —*Niccolo Machiavelli*

Puzzle 336

Cryptic Clue: Environmentally friendly emerald (5)

Puzzle 337

Cryptic Clue: Overcome the overlord (6)

Chapter 13
Double Level Puzzles

Puzzle 338

Difficulty Level: Treacherous

Solve this cipher to reveal the keyword for Puzzle 339.

FGW HGJKRVDHPG IW IOHDHJS

JRGDOHRJ DSFD EHJVPTRORE DSHJ

URJJFLR ZPCNE SFTR ORJCNDRE HG

SRO IRHGL SFGLRE FJ F JKW ZHDSHG

F ARZ EFWJ, NRFTHGL SRO IPWJ

POKSFGJ.

Puzzle 339

Difficulty Level: Treacherous

The keyword from Puzzle 338 will help you crack this Rail Fence Cipher!

INOYI EYIWH SOLTE AECOM RLLAR TNBLC SNTOS SEWEN
GARAH FHTFR MAPRR LRTBI ILEOR GHBIE IHRLO DAKTR
TSFEE MUSAN ATESL IHNEW TRTNR OEYOT PEFUT HODHE
CEHHT VIITW TOOIET

Puzzle 340

Difficulty Level: Treacherous

Find the keyword hidden in this encrypted message and unlock Puzzle 341.

Σηε ηαδ σεντ ονε οφ ηερ οων ψουνγ βοψσ υπ αηεαδ όφ ηερ ατ γρεατ όπεεδ το φινδ με ανδ αλερτ με το τηε νεεδ φορ ιμμεδιατε δεπαρτυρε. Ηοωεϖερ, ηερ χηιλδ χόυλδ νοτ φινδ με, ασ I ωασ μεετινγ ανοτηερ αγεντ βψ αππουίντμεντ.

Puzzle 341

Difficulty Level: Treacherous

Use the keyword revealed in Puzzle 340 to determine the correct order of columns of letters in this Columnar Transposition Cipher. (Check out the instructions on how to solve these ciphers in Chapter 2.)

Any repeated letters in the keyword are ignored (so CARNATION would be written as CARNTIO, without the second A and N).

SEHED TIERM NOEDT GROHE STELF HGROU HMENE YELIN
SETOG TSTHI UNRGE TSMES AOGET MRAJO TMALL AXDGE

Puzzle 342

Difficulty Level: Treacherous

Find the keyword hidden in this encrypted message and unlock Puzzle 343.

GVPABJA RDEN OLI FBTI ER LID

WCFYIO CJP OLI UECP BO OLIJ

SCDDBIP, B ZEVUP AVIFF OLCO FLI

LCP ABHIJ CZCM CWEVO LCUR OLI

WCFYIO CF ABROF OE FIJODBIF CO

HCDBEVF SLISYQEBJOF.

Puzzle 343

Difficulty Level: Treacherous

This is a Twisted Path Cipher. The keyword from Puzzle 342 helps you solve it. We broke the message into five-letter pieces, just to increase the challenge!

ANRIS KEDHE RLMIN GTOGE TTHIO ETOYO UIAMF WBEBR
AVERI SESLG RYXKJ YNCAI LAEHF OEWAR NHESS EMLAI
CUDTW SYLIM AFREH

Puzzle 344

Difficulty Level: Treacherous

Find the keyword hidden in this encrypted message (it's also the blank word). It will unlock Puzzle 345.

NKVUBRZ JS JUA OBJDUAR, B QXJ SR

JUA KQCSR SP K VACHBRZ ZBCT, KRN

KCCKRZAN JS JKOA JUA QTKDA SP

JUA VACHC PSC UBV JKITA. VXCA

ARSXZU, JUACA EKV KRSJUAC LKR

EUS UKN FSBRAN GSXC DSLQKRBSR.

B JSSO JUABC SCNAC, KRN JUAR UBN

BR JUA RAWJ ISSJU JS TBVJAR. B

UAKCN SRTG K PAE ESCNV:

"_ _ _ _ _ _" EKV QCSLBRARJ KLSRZ

JUAL, KV EKV JUA ESCN "CAQTKDA."

Puzzle 345

Difficulty Level: Treacherous

Use the keyword revealed in Puzzle 344 to determine the correct order of columns of letters in this Columnar Transposition Cipher.

OODINT WONKWH HSTACE HSEMTE NMESEH NEVAIT
NLEHOG UNURBT ETNIHS TROHTH AMYEEN AUOYHR
EEBMVR EACYRF ADLUER OENOXX

Puzzle 346

Difficulty Level: Treacherous

Find the keyword hidden in this encrypted message and
unlock Puzzle 347.

UCAFVCH JDGA QDCC OA PN SACJ MN

ZY. QA YSFCC SFTA MN XFGA RN QDMS

NZV NQP RATDUAY DP YFIALZFVRDPL

MSA LNCR. QA SFTA MSA XAFPY MN

OZVH DM RAAJ QDMSDP MSA SDCC

UNZPMVH DP MSA YNZMS, NZM DP

MSA QAYM, NZM QSAVA MSA

JNJZCFMDNP DP YUFVUA FPR

YHXJFMSH INV MSA UFZYA DY SDLS.

FPR MSAP QA'CC QFDM.

Puzzle 347

Difficulty Level: Treacherous

The keyword from Puzzle 346 helps you crack this Rail Fence
Cipher!

IOTES OMBEH OCRCT ATUIH NCNIR POAAL HLTBL GIATA
IASAX MNCWC NTONU EHYEE OPIOH ITNST GSINE IHOIE
WBTWT SDESC

Puzzle 348

Difficulty Level: Treacherous

Find the keyword hidden in this encrypted message and unlock Puzzle 349.

ATD DHG NIT YOECRHHOW DEO

ARSTHL ZR VRME RNNTAO DZ ZBTC

XOEV SRSOHZ. VRM PTWW

GONTHTZOWV IO DEEOCZOG. T DS

HRZ CMEO, IMZ TN ZBOV BDXO

OHRMLB ZR DEEOCZ VRM, ZBOV

YERIDIWV BDXO OHRMLB ZR ARHXTAZ

VRM.

Puzzle 349

Difficulty Level: Treacherous

This is a Twisted Path Cipher. The keyword from Puzzle 348 helps you solve it.

ISOSAIMMEVEI MROYTEOEATTE RTTEHSXHHANM
YHHARTUEHTOE ATSOROCTRSYI TCFEYYLUUEWS
OEMSALSOAOTT MEPNITYRNHEO SEIPEOSOEMUI
TDEDTAGTISET

Puzzle 350

Difficulty Level: Treacherous

Find the keyword hidden in this Caesar Cipher, and then use it
to unlock Puzzle 351.

IO IPVUO. YLT CVUO JDKTSOQ, JVYIO

ETQS QORLKGQ.

Puzzle 351

Difficulty Level: Treacherous

Use the keyword revealed in Puzzle 350 to determine
the correct order of columns of letters in this Columnar
Transposition Cipher.

FOEFI PMEYR NSAOR NCGOL UALTR OTNIA YOONS ARPCU
EUORT ETTHF TAOIR NMNAR MEYIH OUNDO NTOKO IMHEW
VWEEO OKWNR IFRAA UMNOA OAUBT UYJOT

Part III

Hints and Answers to the Cryptos and Codes

The 5th Wave   By Rich Tennant

"That's 3 'Genius Level Puzzle Books' at $8.95 each. Okay, I'll give you a $20, two $5's and 19¢. No wait, I'll give you two $20's and a dime and you give me a nickel back... no I'll keep the nickel and give you 11¢ plus the two $10's and a $20... no, wait..."

In this part . . .

If you get stuck when trying to solve the puzzles, check out the hints in Chapter 14. And, of course, *after* (ahem) you solve the puzzles, you can check your solutions against the answers in Chapter 15.

Chapter 14

Hints to Help Crack the Cryptograms and Puzzles

In This Chapter

▶ Find a hint for every puzzle in the book

▶ Use the hints when you get stuck

 When you have a hint like A = B, for example, the letter on the left is the ciphertext letter, and the letter on the right is the plaintext letter. (See Chapter 2 for details about these terms.)

Chapter 4

Puzzle 1: U = O

Puzzle 2: D = W

Puzzle 3: L = C

Puzzle 4: F = B

Puzzle 5: I = G

Puzzle 6: X = K

Puzzle 7: V = N

Puzzle 8: E = Y

Puzzle 9: Y = W

Puzzle 10: Q = L

Puzzle 11: N = P

Puzzle 12: T = C

Puzzle 13: F = H

Puzzle 14: E = C

Puzzle 15: L = R

Puzzle 16: E = F

Puzzle 17: X = V

Puzzle 18: N = O

Puzzle 19: F = D

Puzzle 20: E = N

Puzzle 21: D = V

Puzzle 22: M = Y

Puzzle 23: N = F

Puzzle 24: Q = V

Puzzle 25: O = R

Puzzle 26: Z = G

Puzzle 27: N = W

Puzzle 28: V = Q

Puzzle 29: B = U

Puzzle 30: X = L

Puzzle 31: X = K

Puzzle 32: Q = R

Puzzle 33: S = H

Puzzle 34: H = S

Puzzle 35: E = D

Puzzle 36: A = Y

Puzzle 37: I = G

Puzzle 38: P = U

Puzzle 39: X = G

Puzzle 40: N = B

Puzzle 41: E = C

Puzzle 42: E = L

Chapter 5

Puzzle 43: 07 = A

Puzzle 44: XIV = N

Puzzle 45: 11 = C

Puzzle 46: 25 = G

Puzzle 47: 23 = D

Puzzle 48: 05 = W

Puzzle 49: 50 = N

Puzzle 50: 12 = S

Puzzle 51: 16 = P

Puzzle 52: 12 = K

Puzzle 53: 56 = N

Puzzle 54: XX = A

Puzzle 55: 16 = Y

Puzzle 56: IV = D

Puzzle 57: 98 = P

Puzzle 58: 64 = C

Puzzle 59: 36 = I

Puzzle 60: 19 = C

Puzzle 61: 61 = Y

Puzzle 62: 15 = L

Puzzle 63: 74 = C

Puzzle 64: 10 = M

Puzzle 65: VIII = F

Puzzle 66: 21 = N

Puzzle 67: 17 = W

Puzzle 68: 35 = V

Puzzle 69: 14 = G

Puzzle 70: 20 = R

Puzzle 71: XII = L

Puzzle 72: 89 = F

Puzzle 73: 73 = Y

Puzzle 74: XIV = S

Puzzle 75: XXIII = N

Puzzle 76: 92 = A

Puzzle 77: XI = L

Puzzle 78: 24 = O

Puzzle 79: 58 = I

Puzzle 80: 09 = C

Chapter 6

Puzzle 81: The second word is HOPE

Puzzle 82: The third word starts with W

Puzzle 83: The first letter is T

Puzzle 84: The black pen = H

Puzzle 85: The first letter is Y

Puzzle 86: The last word starts with C

Puzzle 87: The last word starts with B

Puzzle 88: The first word is AND

Puzzle 89: The last letter is N

Puzzle 90: The first word starts with B

Puzzle 91: The third word starts with Y

Puzzle 92: The first letter is B

Puzzle 93: The last word starts with A

Puzzle 94: The final letter is T

Puzzle 95: The first letter is C

Puzzle 96: The second word starts with H

Puzzle 97: The second letter in the first word is H

Puzzle 98: The second word starts with T

Puzzle 99: The last word starts with M

Puzzle 100: The last letter is N

Puzzle 101: The second word starts with K

Puzzle 102: .-.-.- = period

Puzzle 103: The last letter is F

Puzzle 104: One of the leaf symbols = L

Puzzle 105: The last letter is F

Puzzle 106: .-.-.- = period, –..– = comma, -....- = dash

Puzzle 107: The last word starts with N

Puzzle 108: The first letter is I

Puzzle 109: The last word is five letters long, and the black dot = D

Puzzle 110: Four words start with S

Chapter 7

Puzzle 111: C = B

Puzzle 112: R = O

Puzzle 113: C = D

Puzzle 114: D = I

Puzzle 115: O = K

Puzzle 116: T = W

Puzzle 117: L = G

Puzzle 118: Q = U

Puzzle 119: M = J

Puzzle 120: L = F

Puzzle 121: P = N

Puzzle 122: M = G

Puzzle 123: F = H

Puzzle 124: K = H

Puzzle 125: Q = F

Puzzle 126: M = R

Puzzle 127: S = B

Puzzle 128: W = M

Puzzle 129: D = K

Puzzle 130: R = M

Puzzle 131: Z = D

Puzzle 132: T = W

Puzzle 133: V = C

Puzzle 134: Q = G

Puzzle 135: L = W

Puzzle 136: S = F

Puzzle 137: K = R

Puzzle 138: Z = R

Puzzle 139: G = L

Puzzle 140: U = N

Puzzle 141: G = P

Puzzle 142: P = Y

Puzzle 143: W = G

Puzzle 144: Q = N

Chapter 8

Puzzle 145: The first word starts with T

Puzzle 146: The second word starts with W

Puzzle 147: D is the last letter

Puzzle 148: The second letter is O

Puzzle 149: R is the final letter

Puzzle 150: One of the double letters is L

Puzzle 151: The third word starts with D

Puzzle 152: The second word starts with N

Puzzle 153: The first letter is W

Puzzle 154: The first letter is R

Puzzle 155: The last word ends with Y

Puzzle 156: The final letter is R

Puzzle 157: The second word starts with F

Puzzle 158: The first letter is H

Puzzle 159: The second word starts with G

Puzzle 160: The last word starts with F

Puzzle 161: The last word starts with P

Puzzle 162: The longest word starts with C

Puzzle 163: The first word starts with H

Puzzle 164: The letter Z appears twice

Puzzle 165: The second word starts with L

Puzzle 166: Part of the keyword is E _ WI _ _

Puzzle 167: The word NO appears

Puzzle 168: The first letter is D

Puzzle 169: The keyword starts with WA

Puzzle 170: Part of the keyword is A _ SC _ _ D

Puzzle 171: The first letter is M

Chapter 9

Puzzle 194: 3-rail

Puzzle 195: 2-rail

Puzzle 196: 3-rail

Puzzle 197: 3-rail

Puzzle 198: 4-rail

Puzzle 199: 4-rail

Puzzle 200: 3-rail

Puzzle 201: 5-rail

Puzzle 202: 5-rail

Puzzle 203: 4-rail

Puzzle 204: 5-rail

Puzzle 205: There are nine points in the top row

Puzzle 206: There are seven points in the top row

Puzzle 207: There are 11 points in the top row

Chapter 10

Puzzle 208: The last word starts with B

Puzzle 209: The second word starts with H

Puzzle 210: 6 = Y

Puzzle 211: , = m

Puzzle 212: L = :

Puzzle 213: The last word starts with F

Puzzle 214: U = &

Puzzle 215: There are two Ys in the message

Puzzle 216: The last word starts with R

Puzzle 217: The last word starts with I

Puzzle 218: The third word has Z in it

Puzzle 219: { = :

Puzzle 220: E = W

Puzzle 221: The third word starts with R

Puzzle 222: The second word starts with H

Puzzle 223: The first word starts with I

Puzzle 224: F = S

Puzzle 225: The last word starts with L

Puzzle 226: ^ = *

Puzzle 227: Q appears once in the message

Puzzle 228: The second-to-last word starts with W

Puzzle 229: The last word starts with B

Puzzle 230: & = Y

Puzzle 231: The second-to-last word starts with A

Puzzle 232: The second word starts with C

Puzzle 233: { = P

Puzzle 234: F = D and & = U

Puzzle 235: The first word starts with L

Chapter 11

Puzzle 236: T = G

Puzzle 237: The answer has four words

Puzzle 238: 7 x 7 grid

Puzzle 239: V = E

Puzzle 240: 7 x 7 grid

Puzzle 241: S = H

Puzzle 242: The answer has four words

Puzzle 243: 9 x 9 grid

Puzzle 244: W = D

Puzzle 245: K = P

Puzzle 246: 10 wide x 9 high grid

Puzzle 247: B = Y

Puzzle 248: 8 x 8 grid

Puzzle 249: 8 wide x 5 high grid

Puzzle 250: 5 x 5 box cipher

Puzzle 251: 7 wide x 8 high grid

Puzzle 252: 10 x 10 grid, start at top-left corner

Puzzle 253: 13 x 13 grid, start in the center square

Puzzle 254: 10 x 10 grid, start from the lower-right corner

Puzzle 255: 10 wide x 16 high grid

Puzzle 256: 9 x 9 grid

Puzzle 257: The answer has 11 letters

Puzzle 258: 7 wide x 6 high grid, start in lower-left corner

Puzzle 259: 6 wide x 9 high grid, start in lower-right corner

Puzzle 260: 9 wide x 5 high grid, start in the top-left corner

Puzzle 261: 7 wide x 15 high grid; the first word is SIMPLY

Puzzle 262: 10 wide x 11 high grid, start in the top-right corner

Puzzle 263: 8 wide x 7 high grid, start in the top-left corner

Puzzle 264: 6 wide x 21 high grid; the keyword = 625143

Puzzle 265: 10 x 10 grid, start at top-left corner

Puzzle 266: 10 x 10 grid

Puzzle 267: 7 x 7 grid, start from the top-right corner

Chapter 12

Puzzle 268: The initial letters are A, A, F, T, and B

Puzzle 269: The words start with O and I

Puzzle 270: *Unruly* is an anagram indicator

Puzzle 271: The three words start with T, C, and B

Puzzle 272: Two words start with O

Puzzle 273: Add a comma after *tree*

Puzzle 274: The second word starts with TH

Puzzle 275: This is a double definition clue

Puzzle 276: The third word starts with B

Puzzle 277: The third letter is V

Puzzle 278: *Chickens* is the base clue

Puzzle 279: The answer starts with F

Puzzle 280: The words start with K, Y, M, S

Puzzle 281: The two words start with G and C

Puzzle 282: Put a comma after *exercise*

Puzzle 283: The last word starts with W

Puzzle 284: *Held* indicates a hidden word

Puzzle 285: The two words start with E and T

Puzzle 286: The answer starts with C and ends with Y

Puzzle 287: The second word ends with D

Puzzle 288: *Cooked* is an anagram indicator

Puzzle 289: Fish is the base clue, and it's a noun

Puzzle 290: The third word starts with B

Puzzle 291: Both words start with O

Puzzle 292: *Mangled* indicates an anagram

Puzzle 293: A is the first letter, E is the last

Puzzle 294: The words start with D and A

Puzzle 295: Put a comma after *mammal*

Puzzle 296: Put a comma between the two words

Puzzle 297: The words start with D, B, W

Puzzle 298: *Broken* indicates an anagram

Puzzle 299: The second word starts with O

Puzzle 300: The words start with D, T, P

Puzzle 301: Two of the words start with F

Puzzle 302: *Don't be scared* is the base clue

Puzzle 303: The third word starts and ends with T

Puzzle 304: *Part of* indicates a hidden word

Puzzle 305: The words start with M, N, F

Puzzle 306: *Jostled* is an anagram indicator

Puzzle 307: This is a hidden word clue

Puzzle 308: The first word ends with P

Puzzle 309: A hidden word clue; ignore the punctuation!

Puzzle 310: The second and sixth words start with S

Puzzle 311: Add a comma after *upright*

Puzzle 312: The third word starts with R and ends with N

Puzzle 313: The first two words start with G and L

Puzzle 314: The words start with M, T, N

Puzzle 315: Add a comma after *widespread*

Puzzle 316: *Agitated* indicates an anagram

Puzzle 317: The initial letters are P, D, T, L

Puzzle 318: *Reveal* indicates a hidden word

Puzzle 319: Put a comma after *in*

Puzzle 320: The words start with S, T, K

Puzzle 321: The words start with A, W

Puzzle 322: *Armed conflict* is the base clue

Puzzle 323: *Damaged* indicates an anagram

Puzzle 324: The last word starts with C and ends with E

Puzzle 325: Two words start with C

Puzzle 326: *Some* and *hold* are hidden word indicators

Puzzle 327: The words start with C and I

Puzzle 328: *Grated* indicates an anagram

Puzzle 329: Put a comma after *group*

Puzzle 330: The words start with I, W, T, K

Puzzle 331: *Broken* refers to an anagram

Puzzle 332: The words start with F, O, M

Puzzle 333: The first word starts with T

Puzzle 334: *Upsetting* indicates an anagram

Puzzle 335: Two words are almost identical

Puzzle 336: Put a comma after *friendly*

Puzzle 337: Put a comma after *overcome*

Chapter 13

Puzzle 338: A = F

Puzzle 339: Seventeen points are in the top row

Puzzle 340: The answer has six letters

Puzzle 341: The grid of letters is 5 columns x 16 rows

Puzzle 342: A = G

Puzzle 343: 12 wide x 8 high grid

Puzzle 344: C = R

Puzzle 345: 6 wide x 16 high grid

Puzzle 346: U = C

Puzzle 347: Fifteen points

Puzzle 348: S = M

Puzzle 349: 12 wide x 10 high grid

Puzzle 350: I = B

Puzzle 351: 5 wide x 22 high grid

Chapter 15

Answers to All Cryptograms and Puzzles

In This Chapter
▶ Look up the answers to every puzzle in the book
▶ Check your work against these answers

Chapter 4

Puzzle 1: I propose that we meet personally to allow me to convey to you my plans, maps, and so forth.

Puzzle 2: We have indeed established your credentials. Please tell me more about what you wish to offer to the service of the army of His Majesty the King.

Puzzle 3: . . . appointed the head of Secret Intelligence for the British military forces who are fighting against the Colonial patriots.

Puzzle 4: General Arnold has been slighted for promotion, accused of diverting military funds for personal use, and otherwise insulted by his associates among the rebel colonists.

Puzzle 5: With the advent of war, the agenda of the Knights must change. Their public activity should focus on "peace," on fanning the flames of sympathy for the South and its cause, on promoting the good sense of slavery.

Puzzle 6: Are you satisfied with a title like Governor — or would something like "Duke" suit you better? Washington would not accept the title of King; I do not have his prejudice against titles of nobility — and neither, I think, do you.

Puzzle 7: Had I been more seen, just a slight bit more visible, among those who were gathering arms for my cause, then that court would have convicted me, all those years ago . . .

Puzzle 8: I have always been interested to hear of your military exploits, and especially to hear of your much less well-known activities involving Kentucky — and the king of Spain.

Puzzle 9: . . . a substantial set of assets that dates back to the Civil War, involving caches of precious metals, particularly gold. We have a general idea of the locations of the metals involved, and can pin down a cache to within a ten mile radius, often less — but that is not much better than knowing nothing.

Puzzle 10: Underneath the welcome mat outside your apartment door, you will find a manila envelope with a file indicating where you can discover evidence of Mr. Halligan's activities.

Puzzle 11: As always, there will be a substantial benefit to you personally as we recover the caches. Please do take more than the usual precautions that your staff suspects nothing. Those who do, I am sorry to say, must be handled with extreme prejudice.

Puzzle 12: Many, many years ago, as a security precaution, several of the operatives of this organization adopted color names as cryptonyms. Perhaps one day you shall be part of our organization, and have such a cryptonym yourself.

Puzzle 13: If you would win a man to your cause, first convince him that you are his sincere friend. Therein is a drop of honey that catches his heart, which, say what he will, is the great highroad to his reason, and which, once gained, you will find but little trouble in convincing him of the justice of your cause, if indeed that cause is really a good one. *Abraham Lincoln*

Puzzle 14: Concealment writing may take a host of forms. Perhaps its oldest known application is found in the ancient device of writing a secret message on the head of a slave and dispatching the slave with his communication after his growing hair had covered the writing. *Helen Fouché Gaines*

Puzzle 15: Thieves respect property. They merely wish the property to become their property that they may more perfectly respect it. *G. K. Chesterton*

Puzzle 16: I can win an argument on any topic, against any opponent. People know this, and steer clear of me at parties. Often, as a sign of their great respect, they don't even invite me. *Dave Barry*

Puzzle 17: I have another way into Clinton's tent, which I have been developing for some time.

Puzzle 18: It would be best to proceed without delay with my plan to turn this stronghold over to His Majesty.

Puzzle 19: . . . confirm that the writer of that message is indeed the esteemed General Arnold, victor of the Battle of Saratoga.

Puzzle 20: . . . Dr. George W. L. Bickley to serve as the leader and nominal founder of that group . . .

Puzzle 21: Doctor Bickley's "invasion" of Mexico was unrelievedly disastrous. Replace him as head of the Knights of the Golden Circle. (Keyword = MEXICO)

Puzzle 22: John Wickham, one of my attorneys, should be known to you as "Orange"; should I not be able to escape my current predicament, you shall report to him. (Keyword = ORANGE)

Puzzle 23: I am an employee in the Directorate of Operations in the Central Intelligence Agency. My supervisor is one Burton Mannheim. My office handles the operations of field operatives — basically, spies — in certain locations around the world. (Keyword = BURTON)

Puzzle 24: You have identified Soviet and other Communist agents at the Departments of State, Defense, Interior, and Transportation . . .

Puzzle 25: I know in particular that you have a strong desire to serve your country, to protect your country from enemy agents, in particular to protect your country from double agents . . .

Puzzle 26: The first obligation of the demonstrator is to be legible. Miss Manners cannot sympathize with a cause whose signs she cannot make out even with her glasses on. *Judith Martin*

Puzzle 27: The world is divided into people who do things and people who get the credit. Try, if you can, to belong to the first class. There's far less competition. *Dwight Morrow*

Puzzle 28: Despite pleas from several of his aides, including Hamilton that André be executed by firing squad as befits a soldier, Washington ordered that he be hanged as a spy. He was not in a sentimental or generous mood. *(Joseph J. Ellis, His Excellency: George Washington, 2008, p. 129)*

Puzzle 29: General Washington, we have in our custody Major John André, out of uniform, who was intercepted near Tarrytown today on the way to British lines. (Keyword = WEST POIN[T])

Puzzle 30: A Commendation Given Under the Hand of George Washington, Commander-in-Chief, The Continental Army. Let all men know by these presents that Mrs. Alice Carroll did risk her life for the cause of freedom in the service of her country The United States of America which is eternally grateful. Though these thanks must be kept secret, our gratitude shall last as long as our freedom.

Puzzle 31: I ask you to give safe passage to my wife Peggy and my children, to Peggy's family in Philadelphia.

Puzzle 32: Your Major André — caught, like Hale, in civilian clothes behind enemy lines — the mark of a spy — shall meet the same fate, by the rules of war. (Keyword = ORDEAL)

Puzzle 33: At the end of his stay in the oasis, the nomad folds his tent and moves away; the caravan disappears from sight, but continues its journey in silence.

Puzzle 34: Jefferson Davis, President, The Confederate States of America

Puzzle 35: I have the blessing of a former commanding officer of yours to communicate to you a request for assistance. If you can spare an hour or two for conversation on a matter of mutual interest, I ask your indulgence to meet me tomorrow night at Heron's Tavern, not far from your lodgings, beginning at eight p.m. (Keyword = TAVERN)

Puzzle 36: Unfortunately, I cannot impede you, either. I have no proof of our conversation. This note will be left in a bottle in a hole in a tree; I have no way to direct the authorities to you. So, all I can do is refuse you, and that I do irrevocably. (Keyword = HOLE)

Puzzle 37: It is crucial that my role in this identification not be mentioned to your colleagues or superiors. I am in an extremely sensitive position that must not be compromised.

Puzzle 38: There was clearly too much of a trail left by the satellite repositioning to have fully covered your tracks. (Keyword = TRACKS)

Puzzle 39: Commendation to Allison Carroll, Whose courage and ingenuity in the face of adversity upheld the finest traditions of both the American intelligence community and her own family. Though this nation's thanks must be kept secret, our gratitude shall last as long as our freedom.

Puzzle 40: A military operation involves deception. Even though you are competent, appear to be incompetent. Though effective, appear to be ineffective. *Sun Tzu (~ 400 BC)*

Puzzle 41: A censor is a man who knows more than he thinks you ought to. *Laurence J Peter*

Puzzle 42: It is a fair summary of history to say that the safeguards of liberty have been forged in controversies involving not very nice people. *Felix Frankfurter*

Chapter 5

Puzzle 43: . . . providing the British with military information about the American patriots' Continental Army, such as the size and location of groups of Continental Army troops.

Puzzle 44: The word that we have from multiple agents placed in the camp of the British, working independently of one another, all points to the same conclusion.

Puzzle 45: Please send us notice as to whether this offer is acceptable to you, along with your plans to turn over West Point.

Puzzle 46: This is a closely guarded secret within the inner circle of General Sir Henry Clinton, a group that my agents cannot penetrate.

Puzzle 47: Oh, yes, I know of the plans that you had to deliver Kentucky to Spain. I know a great many things that are not widely known, including your secret renunciation of American citizenship, the oath of allegiance that you made to the Spanish throne, and the annual pension that you receive from Madrid.

Puzzle 48: With the conviction of Vallandigham this week for "uttering disloyal sentiments", we need to change tactics and strategize for the larger picture.

Puzzle 49: I am discovered, and that Wilkinson is set to testify against me. None of the rest of you are known, and so it shall remain.

Puzzle 50: . . . Bickley must think that the establishment of the Knights of the Golden Circle is his own brainchild.

Puzzle 51: Mr. Halligan has been serving as a double agent for the Soviet Union for many years, in which position he has compromised many delicate diplomatic negotiations.

Puzzle 52: I know that retasking intelligence satellites over American soil is a sensitive issue. I suggest that you retask the satellites in such a way that they have to fly over American territory to other locations; the scans can then be performed in passing, as it were.

Puzzle 53: . . . they discovered the new evidence that I planted in Halligan's home and office, as they had discovered what I planted earlier in the month.

Puzzle 54: The call you picked up this afternoon, when someone asked for a nonexistent office, was placed by one of my associates; the record of that call will substantiate your story about an anonymous telephone tip.

Puzzle 55: It takes your enemy and your friend, working together, to hurt you to the heart: the one to slander you and the other to get the news to you. *Mark Twain*

Puzzle 56: If a secret piece of news is divulged by a spy before the time is ripe, he must be put to death together with the man to whom the secret was told. *Sun Tzu*

Puzzle 57: Propaganda: that branch of the art of lying which consists in very nearly deceiving your friends without quite deceiving your enemies. *Francis M Cornford*

Puzzle 58: The public say they are getting cynical about politicians; they should hear how politicians talk about them. *George Weldon*

Puzzle 59: . . . properly accounting for his expenses while fighting in Canada, even though Arnold's receipts were lost in battle.

Puzzle 60: . . . circumstances are such as to compel me to reconsider my position. I now wish to broach the possibility of changing my allegiance to the side of His Majesty the King.

Puzzle 61: You will immediately send patrols to search without raising alarm the area from West Point, south past Tarrytown, from September twenty-first through the twenty-ninth.

Puzzle 62: You, and the rest of the Spectrum agents — Red, Yellow, Blue, Orange, and all the rest — as well as myself are the Inner Circle.

Puzzle 63: What a dramatic death! As an attorney for the defense in a murder case, Clement tries to re-enact the shooting in an attempt to show how the victim had actually shot himself by accident — and Clement proceeds to shoot himself by accident!

Puzzle 64: The man by whom I send this message shall be your liaison with me.

Puzzle 65: After a few years of field experience, with your FBI record of catching double agents, you would be a natural for a transfer to the office of the Directorate of Intelligence that focuses on counterintelligence.

Puzzle 66: . . . not to print off the computer screen on which my messages appear. Your careful attention to follow detailed instructions as dictated to you makes you a very valuable asset in any organization.

Puzzle 67: The worst government is often the most moral. One composed of cynics is often very tolerant and humane. But when fanatics are on top there is no limit to oppression. *H L Mencken*

Puzzle 68: History teaches us that men and nations behave wisely once they have exhausted all other alternatives. *Abba Eban*

Puzzle 69: There are a terrible lot of lies going around the world, and the worst of it is half of them are true. *Winston Churchill*

Puzzle 70: I courted one Miss Peggy Shippen while I was stationed in Philadelphia. This would be the same Peggy Shippen who is your wife.

Puzzle 71: As a gentleman myself, of course I give safe passage to your wife and family.

Puzzle 72: You have no reputation to defend. Your family will suffer the ignominy you have brought upon your name, for now, and for always.

Puzzle 73: Yes, the Southern Jurisdiction of the Scottish Rite has facilities here and there throughout many states and territories of the country . . .

Puzzle 74: Henceforth, have the public organization known as the "Order of the Sons of Liberty".

Puzzle 75: No doubt you will find it surprising to see me communicate with you in cipher. I assure you that my intentions are most honorable.

Puzzle 76: It was not a happy face I saw. I saw your countenance grow darker and darker, though you said very little. When you left, I saw that your companion was somewhat displeased, as well.

Puzzle 77: Your role in getting unauthorized intelligence to me has been exposed — I don't know by whom.

Puzzle 78: Honor and Duty are the pole-stars of a Mason . . . by never losing sight of which he may avoid disastrous shipwreck. *Albert Pike, Morals and Dogma*

Puzzle 79: Interest in cryptography is not restricted to governments and professional spies. Everybody enjoys a secret. *Martin Gardner*

Puzzle 80: Confidant, Confidante, *n.* One entrusted by A with the secrets of B, confided by him to C. *Ambrose Bierce*

Chapter 6

Puzzle 81: I hope to hear from this source soon.

Puzzle 82: . . . I visited West Point, and I took careful note of several ways in which the defenses of this fortification can be weakened to allow His Majesty's Army to take this stronghold without loss.

Puzzle 83: Tonight at dinner, under the influence of some spirituous liquors . . .

Puzzle 84: . . . the British over the financial compensation he would receive.

Puzzle 85: You have access to some of the assets that we accumulated so many years ago, and many contacts. I shall leave it to you to bring about what dreams you can.

Puzzle 86: . . . found a new land, one in the south and the southwest, one built on cotton and sugar, on tobacco and coffee . . .

Puzzle 87: Despite the brave face that I put on events in public, as I mentioned briefly during our conversation, the war goes badly.

Puzzle 88: And, having accepted that unhappy possibility, we must do what can be done to prepare for the next conflict — for a next conflict there must be.

Puzzle 89: . . . whether you are the kind of man whom I can trust with this kind of information. If so, I will have more such information to share. If not, I shall never communicate with you again.

Puzzle 90: Because the caches themselves are in lightly populated hill country or outright wilderness areas, there should be relatively little interference to obscure the gravitometric signal.

Puzzle 91: . . . who serve your enemies while serving in positions of trust in American intelligence and law enforcement.

Puzzle 92: Be faithful . . . to the promises you make, to the pledges you give, and to the vows that you assume, since to break either is base and dishonorable. . . . Be faithful to your country, and prefer its dignity and honor to any degree of popularity and honor for yourself; consulting its interest rather than your own . . . *Albert Pike, Morals and Dogma*

Puzzle 93: I seek in particular a British officer, one Major John André.

Puzzle 94: You have clearly learned of my plans. I can only say that I did what I did for my country — although it may not seem so at the moment.

Puzzle 95: . . . compared her beauty to that of the silver moon at the full, for clarity, for brilliance, and for her beauty's ability to stir the very soul of man.

Puzzle 96: I have entrusted this to you as the walls collapse around me.

Puzzle 97: Their private activity should focus on giving aid to the South, to discouraging enlistment in the Northern Army, even to sabotage in the North.

Puzzle 98: Let's take the name change a bit further, and identify with the original American Revolution.

Puzzle 99: For the good of the country, I beg you, do not ignore this message.

Puzzle 100: Money couldn't buy friends but you got a better class of enemy. *Spike Milligan*

Puzzle 101: I know that's a secret, for it's whispered everywhere. *William Congreve*

Puzzle 102: Defectors are like grapes. The first pressings from them are the best. The third and fourth lack body. *Maurice Oldfield*

Puzzle 103: . . . an intermediary between several of Major Tallmadge's agents in Manhattan and Major Tallmadge himself.

Puzzle 104: He is, after all, an officer in His Majesty's Army, and no common spy.

Puzzle 105: You cannot claim the status of gentleman yourself.

Puzzle 106: Second, I disagree with your means. You wish me to safeguard the Confederate gold to provide for another war. In essence, you have asked me to betray the oath of loyalty that I took to the Union upon the cessation of hostilities in the War Between the States. You clearly have no notion of the importance of an oath to a man such as me. An oath once taken must be fulfilled. Honor and duty are the pole stars of life. I would no more countenance breaking my oath than I would hanging myself — indeed, the latter would be the more honorable course.

Puzzle 107: But I know of a man who might be able to help you — formerly one of our generals, now in the nation's capital. Although by vocation an attorney, he has a powerful position as the head of a large fraternal organization with branches throughout the country outside the Northeast.

Puzzle 108: Incidentally, my internal telephone directory for the FBI in Washington is out of date. Please pass me a current directory at your convenience.

Puzzle 109: Don't worry about Loretta or the children. We'll take care of them. Spare them the agony of a trial. Now is the time to do the expedient thing.

Puzzle 110: Be subtle! Be subtle! And use your spies for every kind of business. *Sun Tzu*

Chapter 7

Puzzle 111: The British are not the only ones with spies on the ground.

Puzzle 112: Major André is now convinced that the would-be traitor is who he says he is.

Puzzle 113: No doubt this message will come to you as something of a surprise.

Puzzle 114: . . . your decision about my compensation.

Puzzle 115: . . . one pulled away from the United States altogether into a benevolent kingdom of its own. You and I can accomplish great things.

Puzzle 116: . . . South Carolina's vote for secession. Open warfare is only months away.

Puzzle 117: The new commander of the Union forces, that General Grant, has a firm grasp of the concept of total war, and he is pursuing that policy most vigorously, not only defeating us on the field of battle, but destroying our capacity to produce even food, wherever he can.

Puzzle 118: Not so. Even during the years of travel that I took in Europe, I knew that I was followed, someone Federal no doubt suspecting that I have accomplices, and seeking to find them.

Puzzle 119: I can tell you about one such agent. His name is Jasper Halligan, an attorney with the United States Department of State.

Puzzle 120: With the single-minded dedication to your profession for which you have become known at the FBI . . .

Puzzle 121: More than any other time in history, mankind faces a crossroads. One path leads to despair and utter hopelessness. The other, to total extinction. Let us pray we have the wisdom to choose correctly. *Woody Allen*

Puzzle 122: What is espionage but the very thing we exercise daily in our lives? *John Le Carré,* attributed

Puzzle 123: You know what charm is: a way of getting the answer yes without having asked any clear question. *Albert Camus*

Puzzle 124: Duty is the moral magnetism which controls and guides the true Mason's course over the tumultuous seas of life. Whether the stars of honor, reputation, and reward do or do not shine, . . . that unerring magnet still shows him the true course to steer . . . To perform that duty, whether the performance be rewarded or unrewarded, is his sole care. And it doth not matter, though of this performance there may be no witnesses, and though what he does will be forever unknown to all mankind. *Albert Pike (Morals and Dogma)*

Puzzle 125: As instructed, I have placed myself under a false name as a serving maid to the officers within the circle of General Clinton.

Puzzle 126: . . . that this offer is truly from the person whose name was signed at the bottom of that message.

Puzzle 127: . . . the maps carry the plain signature of General Benedict Arnold. Please advise us regarding both Major André and General Arnold.

Puzzle 128: He shall make arrangements to put a great deal of the material assets of the Confederacy in your hands.

Puzzle 129: Bickley must make it apparent to all that the heavily agricultural interests in this area — including Cuba, Haiti, Mexico and all of Central America — requires the entry of these territories into the United States as slave territories. Of our later ambitions for that region, you shall say nothing to Bickley.

Puzzle 130: My intermediary shall see to it that you take possession of the last of the gold immediately.

Puzzle 131: Your young prospect, Special Agent Mannheim, was permitted to lead the team to arrest this Halligan fellow at State. They found Halligan dead, having taken his cyanide pill.

Puzzle 132: People who make history know nothing about history. You can see that in the sort of history they make. *G K Chesterton*

Puzzle 133: This contract is so one-sided that I am surprised to find it written on both sides of the paper. *Lord Evershed*

Puzzle 134: Truth is suppressed, not to protect the country from enemy agents but to protect the Government of the day against the people. *Roy Hattersley*

Puzzle 135: You will with all due haste have your agents in New York City, behind British lines, take former General Benedict Arnold into custody by force, and return him to my camp.

Puzzle 136: For the sake of my reputation and my innocent family, can we not keep this between ourselves?

Puzzle 137: I shall make no exchange for Major André unless it be for Benedict Arnold.

Puzzle 138: After the death of Clement Vallandigham this past June, I lost my last tenuous link to your organization.

Puzzle 139: I understand the terrible predicament you are in: guardian of a vast fortune in gold, scattered about the country, yet being without the means to safeguard it adequately. (Keyword = FORTUNE)

Puzzle 140: This will also help cover the fact that Vallandigham runs all of this from Canada. Make sure he thinks it is his idea.

Puzzle 141: Last night, I happened to be in Heron's Tavern, in the upstairs room, working on my sculpture of the head of the Chamber of Commerce.

Puzzle 142: The enemy's spies who have come to spy on us must be sought out, tempted with bribes, led away and comfortably housed. Thus they will become converted spies and available for our service. *Sun Tzu*

Puzzle 143: So long as men worship the Caesars and Napoleons, Caesars and Napoleons will duly arise and make them miserable. *Aldous Huxley*

Puzzle 144: Good manners are a collection of intelligence, education, taste, and style mixed together so that you don't need any of these things. *P. J. O'Rourke*

Chapter 8

Puzzle 145: . . . terms of compensation . . .

Puzzle 146: . . . proceed with the suitable arrangements.

Puzzle 147: . . . it was an autumn evening, in the churchyard of St. Andrew's Church, of the Church of England.

Puzzle 148: . . . working with diligence to infiltrate this group.

Puzzle 149: . . . more formally an organization with an inner circle, on the one hand, and an outer circle that knows next to nothing about that inner circle, on the other.

Puzzle 150: I suggest that you consider Clement Vallandigham, soon or in the near future; his political connections will be valuable.

Puzzle 151: With the death of Wilkinson in Mexico City last year, I had hoped that the pressure would have lifted from me.

Puzzle 152: The name of our public organization, "Knights of the Golden Circle", smacks too much of the British orders of nobility.

Puzzle 153: . . . which I am slipping out with a renewal notice to the Scottish Rite magazine in the name of my deceased grandfather — then they can bring it to the attention of the right people.

Puzzle 154: Rather, use the contents to develop your own investigation and your own evidence. If necessary, you may say that you received an anonymous but untraceable tip by telephone.

Puzzle 155: My message will be much more shocking. I am in desperate straits and I look to you to help, not just me, but your country.

Puzzle 156: I have every reason to believe that your code of honor encourages you to help me, a stranger in need, in this dark hour.

Puzzle 157: A Freemason, therefore, should be a man of honor and of conscience, preferring his duty to everything beside, even to his life; independent in his opinions, and of good morals; submissive to the laws, devoted to humanity, to his country, to his family; kind and indulgent to his brethren, friend of all virtuous men, and ready to assist his fellows by all means in his power. *Albert Pike, Morals and Dogma*

Puzzle 158: Having violated that oath, you are no longer my brother, as a Mason or otherwise.

Puzzle 159: . . . former General Arnold evaded my agents, apparently by accident.

Puzzle 160: As we are both members of a society of gentlemen, perhaps this incident can be forgotten.

Puzzle 161: The time for us to establish a public face has come. You will establish that face as soon as possible.

Puzzle 162: In the best of circumstances, we shall simply repossess that . . .

Puzzle 163: Have Vallandigham disband the Order of the Sons of Liberty. We shall now be completely submerged.

Puzzle 164: We have long suspected that he has ordered unauthorized "side operations," small jobs that piggy-backed on authorized operations. However, such suspicions are hard to prove.

Puzzle 165: My late grandfather, Wilford Carroll, was a Freemason, and a member of the Scottish Rite. Upon his death last year, I inherited some of his effects, including some books that gave details of some old ciphers used in the Scottish Rite over a century ago — one of which I am using here.

Puzzle 166: I strongly suspect that my electronic and telephone communications are being monitored. I cannot directly contact the personnel within CIA who could help me with this matter. (Keyword = EDWINA)

Puzzle 167: The chief distinction of a diplomat is that he can say no in such a way that it sounds like yes. *Lester Bowles Pearson*

Puzzle 168: Democracy is the recurrent suspicion that more than half of the people are right more than half of the time. *E. B. White*

Puzzle 169: . . . the agents cannot betray one another, and I am unlikely ever to be caught and hanged as a spy. The system generally worked well . . . (Keyword = WASHINGTO[N])

Puzzle 170: . . . on Great Jones Street, my agents converged there, only to find that but a few hours earlier he had removed himself suddenly to another location. (Keyword = ABSCOND)

Puzzle 171: . . . Mrs. Carroll is not trained as a courier. Although a widow, she is not much older than a girl herself.

Puzzle 172: The end is now just a matter of time. The time has come to activate our preparations, to protect our assets for some future generation.

Puzzle 173: Second, I feel myself watched as if by hawks, by Union agents who would soon detect any attempt to set up an organization. (Keyword = PIKE)

Puzzle 174: First, I disagree with your aims, most vigorously. The empire that you propose be built on slavery would be a cancerous tumor on a continental scale. Slavery is a disease, an evil, bred from concern that values profit over humanity. Like all diseases, and all evils, slavery comes with consequences. Those who wrote their tolerance of slavery into the Constitution ensured the bloodbath of the War Between the States as readily as if they had staged that war themselves.

Puzzle 175: As long as I have known him, Mr. Mannheim has occasionally made unusual requests of his staff, both here and abroad.

Puzzle 176: Two of my colleagues who were bold enough to voice suspicions about this have been suddenly 'transferred', although no one seems to know where.

Chapter 9

Puzzle 177: . . . give support to His Majesty's Army.

Puzzle 178: . . . American would-be traitor

Puzzle 179: . . . commander of the Continental Army forces at West Point.

Puzzle 180: Your terms are acceptable.

Puzzle 181: The existence of the Inner Circle must remain invisible to him.

Puzzle 182: . . . charges of treason . . .

Puzzle 183: Let the Northeast have its swollen cities and its factories.

Puzzle 184: . . . be the hidden hand, not the public face.

Puzzle 185: You do not know me. I, however, know a fair amount about you.

Puzzle 186: . . . the manila envelope and its contents.

Puzzle 187: Diplomacy — lying in state. *Oliver Herford*

Puzzle 188: Alice Carroll

Puzzle 189: . . . variety of plans and maps relating to West Point.

Puzzle 190: . . . give my love to my cousin Charles.

Puzzle 191: . . . this asset shall finance the next conflict.

Puzzle 192: How good of you it is to contact me after all these years.

Puzzle 193: Change the name to "Order of the American Knights," working through Vallandigham's aides.

Puzzle 194: Do not present the contents of the manila envelope to your associates.

Puzzle 195: You may be assured that your application for the CIA will be given expeditious treatment.

Puzzle 196: . . . this message will disappear from your screen within ten seconds of your reaching the last line.

Puzzle 197: Gentlemen do not read each other's mail. *Henry Stimson*

Puzzle 198: Anarchism is a game at which the police can beat you. *George Bernard Shaw*

Puzzle 199: Have we established my credentials?

Puzzle 200: I appeal to you as a brother Mason.

Puzzle 201: The agents never meet each other or him.

Puzzle 202: Although we never met, I expect that he remains a true son of the Confederacy.

Puzzle 203: Surely someone within the Scottish Rite in this area is affiliated with the CIA.

Puzzle 204: . . . exchange my Major John André for General Benedict Arnold.

Puzzle 205: A little rebellion now and then is a good thing. *Thomas Jefferson*

Puzzle 206: I hate to spread rumors, but what else can one do with them? *Amanda Lear*

Puzzle 207: Something unpleasant is coming when men are anxious to tell the truth. *[Benjamin] Disraeli*

Chapter 10

Puzzle 208: . . . to what did I compare her beauty?

Puzzle 209: I have this day received my commission as commander of West Point.

Puzzle 210: . . . rebuked by both Congress and General Washington . . .

Puzzle 211: I am authorized to make you a final offer of 20,000 pounds.

Puzzle 212: . . . agitating for American expansion into the Golden Circle of a 1,000 mile radius, centered on Havana.

Puzzle 213: My meetings with the British representatives go well, although yet without fruit.

Puzzle 214: . . . heart to see the opportunities that this continent offers to men of vision and strength of will.

Puzzle 215: This shall be my last message to you.

Puzzle 216: If you simply get this message to someone at the CIA, they will take care of verifying the rest.

Puzzle 217: However, I've recently become aware of the work of someone whom you might find of interest.

Puzzle 218: . . . focusing on neutralizing the efforts of the enemies of the nation to spy on America.

Puzzle 219: One final tip to rebels: always have a second profession in reserve. *Nigel Nicolson*

Puzzle 220: . . . let slip that his chief of spies, Major John André, would be meeting with a well-placed traitor just south of West Point, on September 21st.

Puzzle 221: Anyone who raises the slightest suspicion is to be detained and searched.

Puzzle 222: She had no part in any of this.

Puzzle 223: . . . imminent war between North and South . . .

Puzzle 224: You shall have our future in your hands, guard it well!

Puzzle 225: I must look ahead to the very real possibility that we shall not prevail — not this time, at least.

Puzzle 226: Suggest you consider Burton Mannheim, currently at FBI National Security Division (hired 15 June 1977), may be our kind of operative

Puzzle 227: Your inquiries are the mark of an independent, searching mind.

Puzzle 228: Truth is beautiful, without doubt; but so are lies. *Ralph Waldo Emerson*

Puzzle 229: History repeats itself; historians repeat one another. *Rupert Brooke*

Puzzle 230: You may recall how a mere boy was hung as a spy in your camp some time ago. The memory of Nathan Hale is still bright among my men.

Puzzle 231: . . . a woman whose true name is Alice Carroll . . .

Puzzle 232: . . . on Chrystie Street too late to mount another attempt on him, before he was brought into the British camp.

Puzzle 233: September 30, 1871

Puzzle 234: . . . redirect one or more of the KGH-15 satellites under your control to do some quick scans of the areas circled on the attached map. The gravitometric capabilities of the KGH-15s should allow you to detect disturbances in the Earth's gravitational field that could be associated with large amounts of a heavy metal, like refined gold. And yes, there is that much. [The shift between the different encryptions happens at *detect*.]

Puzzle 235: Lies are like children: They're hard work, but it's worth it because the future depends on them. *Pam Davis*

Chapter 11

Puzzle 236: Major André is shocked. This is an offer of treason from a major figure within the Army of the colonists, fighting against the British crown!

Puzzle 237: . . . proposes to change sides . . .

Puzzle 238: My plans are too extensive to outline in a ciphered message.

Puzzle 239: Lesson to the modern executive: Always hang on to your receipts!

Puzzle 240: Of the actual inner circle, he must know absolutely nothing.

Puzzle 241: I agree with you: Watch Wilkinson. He is not entirely to be trusted. However, his ongoing associations in Madrid and Mexico City may be useful to us.

Puzzle 242: The Union naval blockade . . .

Puzzle 243: Wilkinson knows me, of course, but he must never even suspect that you have a direct connection to me.

Puzzle 244: I strongly recommend that you apply for a position within the Central Intelligence Agency, within the Directorate of Operations. (That would be the spies.)

Puzzle 245: Sorry to be out of touch for so long. As I approach retirement, the opportunity to share information with you has been diminishing for some time.

Puzzle 246: If you think cryptography is the answer to your problem, then you don't know what your problem is. *Peter Neumann* [quoted in *The New York Times,* February 20, 2001]

Puzzle 247: In cyberspace everyone will be anonymous for fifteen minutes. *Graham Greenleaf*

Puzzle 248: . . . outside that Quaker meetinghouse in Philadelphia, one fine summer's evening?

Puzzle 249: General Arnold decides to change sides for sure.

Puzzle 250: . . . the identity of the traitor.

Puzzle 251: The day darkens about us. Atlanta fell to the Union forces yesterday.

Puzzle 252: That dream of mine, a golden circle of empire, is simply not to be. It must be for another age, another group of men with vision.

Puzzle 253: Emerald: Police were waiting near the tree. Retrieved Pike's message but was nearly caught myself. Looks like plainclothes detectives are on the streets looking for me. Suggest we fall back to Arlington now.

Puzzle 254: Recently, Mr. Mannheim went so far as to redirect surveillance satellites and collect data over the United States itself.

Puzzle 255: Few false ideas have more firmly gripped the minds of so many intelligent men than the one that, if they just tried, they could invent a cipher that no one could break. *David Kahn, The Codebreakers*

Puzzle 256: It is always the best policy to tell the truth — unless, of course, you are an exceptionally good liar. *[Jerome K. Jerome]*

Puzzle 257: *The Art of War* [by Sun Tzu]

Puzzle 258: I wish to arrange another exchange for Major André.

Puzzle 259: A true professional, she gave no sign of recognition to me at all.

Puzzle 260: I write this from aboard His Majesty's Ship, the Vulture.

Puzzle 261: . . . simply set out walking down the road to Patriot lines with a basket of fruit, under which she carried her ciphered message to you.

Puzzle 262: I must confess, I wondered then, and wonder today, whether it was one of your people who put that loaded pistol in his unknowing hand.

Puzzle 263: Relative to the larger picture, as we discussed: Prepare to submerge.

Puzzle 264: In theory, yes, it would be possible for the Scottish Rite, SJ, to safeguard the assets of the old Confederacy. However, this will not happen, for two reasons.

Puzzle 265: As a matter of fact, I represent an independent organization altogether, with offices and interests internationally.

Puzzle 266: He trusted neither of them as far as he could spit, and he was a poor spitter, lacking both distance and control. *P. G. Wodehouse*

Puzzle 267: Put all your eggs in one basket and WATCH THAT BASKET. *M Twain*

Chapter 12

Puzzle 268: AN AGENT FOR THE BRITISH

Puzzle 269: OVERTHROW IT

Puzzle 270: FACE (anagram of CAFÉ)

Puzzle 271: THE CONSPIRACY BEGINS

Puzzle 272: THOSE WHO OWN ONE

Puzzle 273: DATE (double definition)

Puzzle 274: DISTORT THEM

Puzzle 275: SUPERIOR (double definition)

Puzzle 276: HAVING A BETTER TIME

Puzzle 277: ADVERSARIES

Puzzle 278: HENS (hidden word)

Puzzle 279: FALSE (anagram of FLEAS)

Puzzle 280: KEEPING YOUR MOUTH SHUT

Puzzle 281: GOLDEN CIRCLE

Puzzle 282: TRAIN (double definition)

Puzzle 283: YOU ARE SPIES; WEAKNESSES

Puzzle 284: DECOY (hidden word)

Puzzle 285: EMERGE TRIUMPHANT

Puzzle 286: CRYPTOGRAPHY

Puzzle 287: THE GOLD

Puzzle 288: MAY (anagram of YAM)

Puzzle 289: TUNA (hidden word)

Puzzle 290: A HARD BATTLE

Puzzle 291: OUR OWN

Puzzle 292: BAGEL (anagram of GABLE)

Puzzle 293: ACCUMULATE

Puzzle 294: DOUBLE AGENT

Puzzle 295: BAT (double definition)

Puzzle 296: CROSS (double definition)

Puzzle 297: DEAR BELOVED WIFE

Puzzle 298: RITES (anagram of TIERS)

Puzzle 299: IS OUTLAWED

Puzzle 300: DENIED THE PRIVILEGE

Puzzle 301: FIND A FOE

Puzzle 302: FEAR NOT (anagram of OAT FERN)

Puzzle 303: IS TO TRUST HIM

Puzzle 304: CIDER (hidden word)

Puzzle 305: MUST NOT FAIL

Puzzle 306: PARIS (anagram of PAIRS)

Puzzle 307: MUSKET (hidden word)

Puzzle 308: KEEP A SECRET

Puzzle 309: BURGUNDY

Puzzle 310: HAD SOMETHING TO DO WITH STAMPS

Puzzle 311: COLUMN (double definition)

Puzzle 312: THAT'S NO REASON NOT TO GIVE IT

Puzzle 313: GOOD LUCK TO US ALL

Puzzle 314: MAINTAIN THEIR NEUTRALITY

Puzzle 315: GENERAL (double definition)

Puzzle 316: MAGENTA (anagram of MAGNATE)

Puzzle 317: PLEASE DESTROY THIS LETTER

Puzzle 318: SPIES (hidden word)

Puzzle 319: LODGE (double definition)

Puzzle 320: SOLOMON THE KING

Puzzle 321: ADMINISTRATIVE WON'T

Puzzle 322: BATTLE (anagram of TABLET)

Puzzle 323: DAGGER (anagram of RAGGED)

Puzzle 324: HE'S NEVER A CANDIDATE

Puzzle 325: CANNOT BUT BE CRUEL

Puzzle 326: CIPHER (hidden word)

Puzzle 327: CRIMINAL INVESTIGATION

Puzzle 328: MEAD (anagram of EDAM)

Puzzle 329: LEAGUE (double definition)

Puzzle 330: INVENTED WEAPONS TO KILL

Puzzle 331: NEW YORK (anagram of WORN KEY)

Puzzle 332: FROM OTHER MEN

Puzzle 333: THIS I MUST DECLINE

Puzzle 334: SHADE (anagram of HADES)

Puzzle 335: TO DECEIVE THE DECEIVER

Puzzle 336: GREEN (double definition)

Puzzle 337: MASTER (double definition)

Chapter 13

Puzzle 338: Any inspection by British sentries that discovered this message would have resulted in her being hanged as a spy within a few days, leaving her boys orphans. (Keyword = FIVE RALS [FIVE RAILS])

Puzzle 339: I came upon Mrs. Carroll nearly at the British line, blithely conversing with two British sentries who were only too glad to partake of the fruit that she offered them.

Puzzle 340: She had sent one of her own young boys up ahead of her at great speed to find me and alert me to the need for immediate departure. However, her child could not find me, as I was meeting another agent by appointment. (Keyword = BOSTON [remove the second O when using this as a keyword in Puzzle 341; that is BOSTN]).

Puzzle 341: . . . she determined to go herself through enemy lines to get this urgent message to Major Tallmadge. (BOSTN = 13452 order for the columns)

Puzzle 342: Judging from the size of her basket and the load it then carried, I would guess that she had given away about half the basket as gifts to sentries at various checkpoints. (Keyword = CW SPIRAL [Clockwise Spiral])

Puzzle 343: This woman risked her life and her family's well-being to get this crucial message to you. I am in awe of her bravery.

Puzzle 344: Dashing to the kitchen, I put on the apron of a serving girl, and arranged to take the place of the server for his table. Sure enough, there was another man who had joined your companion. I took their order, and then hid in the next booth to listen. I heard only a few words: "Kidnap" was prominent among them, as was the word "replace." (Keyword = KIDNAP = 432516 order for the columns in Puzzle 345)

Puzzle 345: I do not know what schemes these men have in the long run, but in the short they mean you harm. Be very careful, dear one.

Puzzle 346: Clearly Pike will be no help to us. We shall have to make do with our own devices in safeguarding the gold. We have the means to bury it deep within the hill country in the South, out in the west, out where the population in scarce and sympathy for the Cause is high. And then we'll wait. (Keyword = FOUR [R]AILS)

Puzzle 347: I am in touch with connections in Europe, who may be able to help with both logistic and strategic assistance.

Puzzle 348: CIA and FBI personnel are coming to your office at this very moment. You will definitely be arrested. I am not sure, but if they have enough to arrest you, they probably have enough to convict you. (Keyword = DIAGON[A]L)

Puzzle 349: I'm sorry to say that the time has come for some extreme steps. You have the cyanide pill that I entrusted to you some years ago. Now is the time to use it.

Puzzle 350: Be brave. You have minutes, maybe just seconds. (Keyword = VIRGO)

Puzzle 351: I offer my personal congratulations on your capture of the traitor Mannheim. You do not know me. I, however, know a fair amount about you . . . (Keyword = VIRGO = 52413 order for the columns)

Appendix

Historical Background to the Conspiracy Stories

*Y*ou may be interested in knowing what's real and what's fantasy in each of the conspiracy stories in Chapter 3.

American General Benedict Arnold really did attempt to turn over West Point to the British. His main contact, British spymaster John André, had actually dated Miss Peggy Shippen before Arnold married her, and Peggy was part of the chain of go-betweens between Arnold and André. Alice Carroll and "the agent known as Solomon the King" are inventions. One of the more famous signers of the Declaration of Independence was named Charles Carroll, however, and Solomon the King is an important character in Masonic mythology.

Not long after the Revolution, Aaron Burr really did conspire, while serving as Vice President of the United States under Thomas Jefferson, to carve out an empire of his own in the American Southwest. Years later, in the decade before the Civil War, the Knights of the Golden Circle did, in fact, conspire to create an agrarian empire based on slavery in a "Golden Circle" centered on Havana. During the Civil War, the Knights actually worked to help the Confederacy. Although some have speculated that they had the assistance of Albert Pike after the Civil War, Pike's actual feelings about slavery and the duty to fulfill an oath fit what is in the story in Chapter 3. Pike did know the sculptress Vinnie Ream, who was working on a bust of Abraham Lincoln at the time of the President's assassination. "Emerald" and his encounter with Pike are inventions.

All the characters and incidents in the "Conspiracy of the Organization" story are made up.

(Or *are* they? *We'll* never tell.)

Business/Accounting & Bookkeeping

Bookkeeping For Dummies
978-0-7645-9848-7

eBay Business
All-in-One For Dummies,
2nd Edition
978-0-470-38536-4

Job Interviews
For Dummies,
3rd Edition
978-0-470-17748-8

Resumes For Dummies,
5th Edition
978-0-470-08037-5

Stock Investing
For Dummies,
3rd Edition
978-0-470-40114-9

Successful Time
Management
For Dummies
978-0-470-29034-7

Computer Hardware

BlackBerry For Dummies,
3rd Edition
978-0-470-45762-7

Computers For Seniors
For Dummies
978-0-470-24055-7

iPhone For Dummies,
2nd Edition
978-0-470-42342-4

Laptops For Dummies,
3rd Edition
978-0-470-27759-1

Macs For Dummies,
10th Edition
978-0-470-27817-8

Cooking & Entertaining

Cooking Basics
For Dummies,
3rd Edition
978-0-7645-7206-7

Wine For Dummies,
4th Edition
978-0-470-04579-4

Diet & Nutrition

Dieting For Dummies,
2nd Edition
978-0-7645-4149-0

Nutrition For Dummies,
4th Edition
978-0-471-79868-2

Weight Training
For Dummies,
3rd Edition
978-0-471-76845-6

Digital Photography

Digital Photography
For Dummies,
6th Edition
978-0-470-25074-7

Photoshop Elements 7
For Dummies
978-0-470-39700-8

Gardening

Gardening Basics
For Dummies
978-0-470-03749-2

Organic Gardening
For Dummies,
2nd Edition
978-0-470-43067-5

Green/Sustainable

Green Building
& Remodeling
For Dummies
978-0-4710-17559-0

Green Cleaning
For Dummies
978-0-470-39106-8

Green IT For Dummies
978-0-470-38688-0

Health

Diabetes For Dummies,
3rd Edition
978-0-470-27086-8

Food Allergies
For Dummies
978-0-470-09584-3

Living Gluten-Free
For Dummies
978-0-471-77383-2

Hobbies/General

Chess For Dummies,
2nd Edition
978-0-7645-8404-6

Drawing For Dummies
978-0-7645-5476-6

Knitting For Dummies,
2nd Edition
978-0-470-28747-7

Organizing For Dummies
978-0-7645-5300-4

SuDoku For Dummies
978-0-470-01892-7

Home Improvement

Energy Efficient Homes
For Dummies
978-0-470-37602-7

Home Theater
For Dummies,
3rd Edition
978-0-470-41189-6

Living the Country
Lifestyle
All-in-One For Dummies
978-0-470-43061-3

Solar Power Your Home
For Dummies
978-0-470-17569-9

Internet
Blogging For Dummies,
2nd Edition
978-0-470-23017-6

eBay For Dummies,
6th Edition
978-0-470-49741-8

Facebook For Dummies
978-0-470-26273-3

Google Blogger
For Dummies
978-0-470-40742-4

Web Marketing
For Dummies,
2nd Edition
978-0-470-37181-7

WordPress For Dummies,
2nd Edition
978-0-470-40296-2

Language & Foreign Language
French For Dummies
978-0-7645-5193-2

Italian Phrases
For Dummies
978-0-7645-7203-6

Spanish For Dummies
978-0-7645-5194-9

Spanish For Dummies,
Audio Set
978-0-470-09585-0

Macintosh
Mac OS X Snow Leopard
For Dummies
978-0-470-43543-4

Math & Science
Algebra I For Dummies
978-0-7645-5325-7

Biology For Dummies
978-0-7645-5326-4

Calculus For Dummies
978-0-7645-2498-1

Chemistry For Dummies
978-0-7645-5430-8

Microsoft Office
Excel 2007 For Dummies
978-0-470-03737-9

Office 2007 All-in-One
Desk Reference
For Dummies
978-0-471-78279-7

Music
Guitar For Dummies,
2nd Edition
978-0-7645-9904-0

iPod & iTunes
For Dummies,
6th Edition
978-0-470-39062-7

Piano Exercises
For Dummies
978-0-470-38765-8

Parenting & Education
Parenting For Dummies,
2nd Edition
978-0-7645-5418-6

Type 1 Diabetes
For Dummies
978-0-470-17811-9

Pets
Cats For Dummies,
2nd Edition
978-0-7645-5275-5

Dog Training For Dummies,
2nd Edition
978-0-7645-8418-3

Puppies For Dummies,
2nd Edition
978-0-470-03717-1

Religion & Inspiration
The Bible For Dummies
978-0-7645-5296-0

Catholicism For Dummies
978-0-7645-5391-2

Women in the Bible
For Dummies
978-0-7645-8475-6

Self-Help & Relationship
Anger Management
For Dummies
978-0-470-03715-7

Overcoming Anxiety
For Dummies
978-0-7645-5447-6

Sports
Baseball For Dummies,
3rd Edition
978-0-7645-7537-2

Basketball For Dummies
2nd Edition
978-0-7645-5248-9

Golf For Dummies,
3rd Edition
978-0-471-76871-5

Web Development
Web Design All-in-One
For Dummies
978-0-470-41796-6

Windows Vista
Windows Vista
For Dummies
978-0-471-75421-3

Available wherever books are sold. For more information or to order direct: U.S. customers visit www.dummies.com or call 1-877-762-2
U.K. customers visit www.wileyeurope.com or call (0) 1243 843291. Canadian customers visit www.wiley.ca or call 1-800-567-4797.